LEADERSHIP UPGRADE

10 Keys to Become the Leader
Your World Is Waiting For

Home. Community. Work.

MICHAEL ROWELL

Copyright © 2021 by Michael Rowell
Leadership Upgrade

All rights reserved. No part of this publication may be reproduced, distributed or transmitted in any form or by any means, including photocopying, recording, or other electronic or mechanical methods, without the prior written permission of the publisher, except in the case of brief quotations embodied in critical reviews and certain other noncommercial uses permitted by copyright law.

Although the author and publisher have made every effort to ensure that the information in this book was correct at press time, the author and publisher do not assume and hereby disclaim any liability to any party for any loss, damage, or disruption caused by errors or omissions, whether such errors or omissions result from negligence, accident, or any other cause.

Neither the author nor the publisher assumes any responsibility or liability whatsoever on behalf of the consumer or reader of this material. Any perceived slight of any individual or organization is purely unintentional.

All stories are a recollection, or combination of similar events, locales and conversations from my memories of them unless otherwise indicated. In order to maintain their anonymity. I have changed the names of individuals and places, as well as some identifying characteristics and details.

Written permission must be obtained from Empowered Nation Publishing for the reproduction or transmission of any part of this publication in any form including recording, photocopying, or by any information storage and retrieval system.

The opening-chapter definitions are taken from Oxford English Dictionary primarily. A few are taken from Merriam-Webster, Dictionary.com. and Collins Online Dictionary.

Empowered Nation Publishing, Sale, Victoria. publishing@empowerednation.com.au

ISBN: 978-0-6451305-0-8 paperback
978-0-6451305-2-2 ebook
978-0-6451305-1-5 hardcover

Visit us at www.empowerednation.com.au.

For bulk orders or speaking engagements, contact the author at michael@empowerednation.com.au.

Cover design: Jeremy Dixon

Editors: Dea Gunning and Margaret Harrell

GET YOUR FREE GIFT!

Get your free copy of
The Leadership Upgrade 10-Day Action Planner—Personal Study Guide!

I've found readers who download and use the study guide as a companion to the book are able to take the next steps to upgrade their leadership faster.

To use the 10 Day Action Planner Study Guide, simply

1. read one chapter of the book per day
2. complete the study-guide questions, assessments and planning guides for that chapter
3. commence your own personally developed action plan to kick-start your *leadership upgrade*—in just 10 days!

PLUS, gain exclusive access to my Leadership Upgrade Facebook community.

To get your free copy, go to
https://empowerednation.com.au/lu-book

This book is dedicated to the select leaders I have had the honour and opportunity to connect with, observe, draw from and follow.

They have modelled the characteristics and principles outlined in this book and are the source and inspiration of its content.

They truly represent the Leadership Upgrade the world is waiting for. I hope this book helps raise up others to travel in their footsteps.

CONTENTS

INTRODUCTION 1

CHAPTER ONE – Integrity 5

CHAPTER TWO – Conviction of Purpose 29

CHAPTER THREE – Vision 53

CHAPTER FOUR – Prioritising Relationships 79

CHAPTER FIVE – Persistence 109

CHAPTER SIX – Leading for Legacy 135

CHAPTER SEVEN – Selfless Service 167

CHAPTER EIGHT – Pioneering Spirit 189

CHAPTER NINE – Breakthrough Thinking 219

CHAPTER TEN – Self-Governance 247

CHAPTER ELEVEN – The Journey Ahead 281

ABOUT THE AUTHOR 287

INTRODUCTION

Leadership changes the world.
If you want to change anything, you've got to be a leader.
And everyone can become a tremendous leader, including you!

While leadership is a lofty title and noble aspiration to reach for, how do we know if our approach is hitting the mark?

Despite our best efforts, we can still fall short in providing effective leadership to our family, our workplace and our community. These environments can still experience decline if we are unable to bring positive transformation.

If we don't have a strong foundation to build our leadership on, or a clear blueprint to guide our future growth, our capacity to lead can be undermined by four main issues:

1. *Incorrect concepts and motivations about the role of a leader*
   The contamination of self-focused mindsets and ambition can distort our leadership endeavours.

2. *Insufficient character development to fulfill the leadership mandate*
   Personal immaturity can limit our capacity to sustain effective leadership.

3. *A lack, or refusal of feedback about the effectiveness of our leadership.*
   Deception regarding the quality of our leadership can infiltrate our perspective.

4. The absence or disconnection from accurate role models
Inaccurate patterns are reproduced from preceding examples.

When any of these four issues affects us, we can be unsure of our identity and purpose, consequently misusing authority. Rather than leading through a purpose driven, others-focused quality of character, we may unknowingly rely on inferior (but all-too-common) approaches, such as the following:

- Power—ruling by authority
- Personality—relying on superficial image
- Popularity—pursuing public approval
- Performance—seeking quick, temporary success
- Pride—elevating self
- Position—dominating by title and status
- Politics—controlling through weight of numbers

There is, however, a solution to escape this toxic cycle.

The answer lies in the realisation that *leaders are made and not born.* The contents of this book will provide you with the essential concepts and understanding of the characteristics you need to avoid these four pitfalls, and increase your leadership capacity, wherever you're starting from today.

This book represents my passion for seeing people reach their potential as leaders in their home, workplace and community.

As you explore the contents you will discover:

- proven principles you can apply to your leadership for immediate results

Introduction

- keys to develop critical traits so you can lead from your character and don't have to rely on your personality.

- how to build a lasting legacy for tomorrow, not just temporary results today.

- how to break though fears, rise above limitations, and lead with purpose and conviction.

- dynamic examples of leaders throughout history, insightful evidence-based research and real-life stories highlighting powerful leadership concepts in action.

Each of the ten chapters introduces a critical leadership characteristic and illustrates its power and impact on our leadership walk. As you read about these vital concepts, I guide you in assessing the current level of your own leadership. I also help you identify areas for growth and give you the tools to develop them moving forward. This book is not a one-time read, but a lifelong resource to continually draw from.

Don't delay. By applying today the blueprints revealed in this book, you can avoid common traps, build your capacity and experience your *leadership upgrade to b*ecome the leader your home, workplace and community is waiting for.

Turn the page to start learning about the first of the ten qualities that will transform your leadership, and read a story about the impact of integrity.

CHAPTER ONE

Integrity

*Integrity: The quality of being honest
and having strong moral principles*

Integrity is a prerequisite for effective leadership.

Integrity, in its simplest form, is when *what we say* matches *what we do*.

If not, our lives resound with a 'hollowness' which people can sense. This will create a hesitancy in them towards us.

---

*Integrity is making sure that the things you say
and the things you do are in alignment.*
—Katrina Mayer

More so than our skills or abilities, our integrity is the bedrock of our leadership.

Charisma and personality go skin deep, but integrity goes right to the core of who we are.

Mark is Viv's husband, and together they have two boys, eleven and eight. Mark earns a modest income, while Viv has worked in a string of casual, temporary administrative positions that are good while they last, but have never been consistent enough to count on. As a result the couple constantly struggle to make ends meet. The financial stress is constant, often escalating the level of conflict in the home, particularly relating to expenses for the children's schooling or sporting activities.

Despite Viv's frequent requests, Mark always resists using an itemised family budget.

Mark insists the exercise would be pointless—as all his pay, he claims, goes toward bills and the mortgage; they just have to watch their optional expenses, he says.

In reality, though, Mark typically spends a substantial amount on extras. He often impulse-buys takeaway food, an hour-long massage and equipment for his tool shed, none of which he reveals to Viv. In itself, spending on these things is not an issue, but Mark's lack of accountability often leaves Viv suspicious and resentful, such as when he arrives home in the evening, not wanting tea because he just had a big meal at a restaurant with colleagues.

Mark's lack of integrity about finances has created distrust in all areas of their relationship, potentially hurting their financial sustainability, and if he tries to offer leadership in other areas of homelife, it decreases his credibility.

When we move towards becoming an 'integrity leader', we act according to our principles. And our actions match our words. Hence, others know what to expect and can identify more strongly with us.[1]

The Impact of Integrity in Leadership

Professor Ronald Burke, who spent forty years studying behaviour in the workplace, published a study titled, 'Why Leaders Fail: Exploring the Dark Side' in the *International Journal of*

Manpower. He demonstrated that more leaders fail because of character-related, integrity issues, such as arrogance, selfishness and betrayal of trust, than from a lack of talent or skills.[2]

Conversely, *Leadership: Theory, Application & Skill Development* authors Robert N. Lussier and Christopher F. Achua state that when a leader's character is established on positive values such as integrity, then followers are more willing to align their beliefs with those of the leader.[3]

Integrity is a critical component of successful leadership.

When we display integrity in our lives, others will understand that with us 'what you see is what you get'. As a result, they are more open to us. When people can see that we are consistent in what we stand for, how we treat people, what our priorities are and what we are motivated by, then we can more likely influence them in a positive manner and they have *the necessary information* to choose to follow us or not.

On the other hand, if we lack integrity, people will likely be sceptical of trusting or following us, for a number of reasons: 1) they're uncertain where we are taking them, or 2) they're fearful that we may be using them or the situation to gain a personal advantage. Most people are not inspired by a leadership vision that revolves around an individual and only benefits the leader.

Internal Alignment—The Starting Point of Integrity

We cannot have integrity in any relationship until we have internal integrity. That is, our thoughts, our emotions, our beliefs, our words and our actions are all consistent and in alignment. If we say we believe one thing but then behave in a way that contradicts that belief, it is only a matter of time before our lack of internal integrity is displayed externally, in a relationship or the public realm.

Integrity and Character

Integrity is not about our skills and abilities. It refers to the state of our character.

That's why an immature or unformed character is often at the heart of integrity issues.

With integrity of character, we continually demonstrate a consistency of character, values and standards, regardless of the people, situations or opportunities we find ourselves in.

When we behave with one set of values and standards with one group, but display a vastly different set of values and standards when mixing with a different crowd, who are we really? This inconsistency demonstrates we can be manipulated. How can people trust or follow us if they don't know who we really are, or who the true 'I' is? When we have integrity, we stick to our standards. We don't adjust our values to fit to what is considered normal or popular.

One of the truest tests of integrity
is its blunt refusal to be compromised.
—Chinua Achebe

The ability to demonstrate integrity through a consistency of character, or not demonstrate it, has significant impact on those connected to us.

Jack is father to twin boys, aged thirteen. He often quickly changes in disposition from calm and funny to angry and aggressive. The slightest thing might set him off. A pair of shoes on the floor inside the house, the outside gate not being closed or the dishwasher not being emptied as requested can flick a switch that sends him from one extreme to the next. His children feel anxious, constantly worried which version of their dad will show up and when Dad may 'snap' again.

Susan is a project manager who—so long as the team is achieving their goals—openly promotes the message that 'we're all in this together'. However, after senior management started investigating her project's unusual patterns of expenditure, which Susan had directed, she quickly steered blame to the project finance officers. Team members felt hurt, quite naturally, that Susan turned on them to protect herself. As a result, they no longer trust her.

Tom, a politician, got elected on his strong stance against the use of nuclear energy. But after changing his views to avoid an adverse public-opinion poll, incensed voters felt he 'sold out'.

If we are not consistent in what we say and do, but demonstrate fluctuating values depending on the situation, it is unlikely people will trust us to any great degree.

Maturing in Integrity

As we mature in integrity, the consistency of our character grows accordingly. The extremes of our highs and lows begin to even out. Likewise, our relationships deepen—are smoother—as those connected to us rely more on the fact they are encountering the 'same person' every time.

Sometimes, however, our immaturity displays our real level of integrity when what's really inside us—despite our shiny, well-polished appearance—is revealed by disappointment (our expectations are not met) or misfortune (things don't pan out as planned). Or, on the other side of the coin, opportunity.

External opportunity and internal ambition are often two catalysts that expose the lack of consistency of character in our heart as leaders.

Sometimes not till those moments do we find out the depth of our integrity and how consistent our character really is. Remember that generally, the integrity of our character is developed and proven over time through victories, defeats, pain, loss and success.

Real-estate agent James had a contact, Lucy, who owned a large parcel of lucrative land zoned for a residential subdivision. James connected Lucy to his property-developer friend Tony, and the three agreed that Tony would manage the subdivision process on Lucy's land, on the condition that James be the realtor to sell the lots.

Close to completion, with the blocks almost ready for sale, however, Tony opened his own real-estate agency to sell the blocks in an exclusive agreement he made with Lucy behind James's back. 'It was too lucrative an opportunity to pass up. Sorry', Tony explained.

We may enjoy a rapid rise to a position of influence or leadership where we are suddenly exposed to new situations, opportunities and temptations that outweigh the stature of our current level of integrity. Our response reveals the true state of our character.

When Penny was appointed Director of Communications, she suddenly had authority to sign off on contracts up to $60 million without seeking department approval. Her parents' long-time family friend, who ran a media corporation, had previously applied for department contracts, but just marginally lacked the necessary skills to be the priority pick.

Now, though, Penny had the capability to appoint contractors at her discretion, and no one would ever ask any questions. However, what did she do? She established a selection committee and referred all applicants for independent review and selection. She was not going to abuse the power of her position by playing favourites and bringing her name or the department into disrepute.

In these situations, resulting from an increase in authority, money or influence, opportunities for personal gain sometimes prove too great for our current level of integrity. We may violate our values, abuse the trust of the group, betray our team or even engage in illegal activity.

> *Nearly all men can stand adversity, but if you want to test a man's character, give him power.*
> —Abraham Lincoln

It doesn't mean we can't grow or develop in our character after these instances if we've failed the integrity test, but it does mean we are vulnerable and need to continue to mature in our level of integrity.

Integrity and Accountability

A characteristic that goes hand in hand with integrity is accountability. Accountability is being responsible for justifying or explaining one's actions.

When we lack or avoid accountability, it automatically raises questions relating to our integrity.

When we can openly volunteer information to relevant people, to explain our actions relating to money, communications or decision-making, and we are willingly transparent, it provides a level of safety and protection for those we connect with. If, on the other hand, we hide information, covering up actions or details, we raise suspicions. It becomes difficult for others to support us wholeheartedly. This is especially true if we have a history of repeated instances of integrity-based issues.

Operating independently and with a lack of accountability, without any checks or balances on what we're doing or how, creates two main issues:

i. Operating in error unknowingly

Firstly, we may be operating in error. If we are lacking accountable relationships or structures, we have no feedback mechanism to warn or protect us from our inaccuracy. Even the most experienced pilot refers to external sources such as the flight tower or the plane's aviation GPS. This confirms the accuracy of their flight path and offers other feedback. Accountable relationships of integrity provide this confirmation to us as leaders, giving us the ability to make corrections and adjustments. If we think that as leaders, we cannot make mistakes or errors of judgement, we place ourselves and those connected to us in danger. History is prolific with examples of strong, but misguided leaders who brought about the demise of themselves, their followers and the broader community due to a lack of accountability.

A lack of accountability from the board of Enron (an American company specialising in energy and commodities trading and services) enabled it to hide substantial financial losses while becoming America's seventh-largest publicly listed company in the year 2000. After an investigation by the Securities and Exchange Commission—and losing many of its clients—in late 2001, Enron filed for bankruptcy.

Its shareholders suffered a loss of $74 billion in the four years its bankruptcy process played out, while 4,500 employees lost their jobs. It appeared the board of directors operated under a culture of group compliance, with unanimous decision-making the norm.

Sometimes, if we do not volunteer accountability, we find it imposed by external forces. As a result of the Enron case, increased accountability was subsequently legislated into US law by the Sarbanes-Oxley Act, which ensured higher levels of disclosure by companies and increased oversight.[4]

ii. Lacking leadership credibility

The second impact of operating without accountability is that if people feel we are merely solo artists, they will be less likely to connect with and follow us. If we're detached from people or groups that can act as 'referees' to validate us, then in the mind of people contemplating joining us, the risk increases.

Critical Areas of Integrity

Two key areas in which we need to develop integrity:

i. Relationships

A crucial question is 'Can people trust me?'

If we tell our family we'll be home at a specific time, commit to completing a task for our boss or make a promise to a community group to volunteer on a particular day, if we have integrity, we will deliver on those words, or explain why we can't.

While some of these examples may seem trivial, if we are untrustworthy with the little things, how will we ever earn trust in the big things? Integrity starts in the fundamental, everyday interactions with those we have relationships with.

If we discredit a person to others when they are not around, no matter how innocently, then we later greet that same person with a cheery smile, we've failed to understand relational integrity.

Integrity is not something you show others.
It is how you behave behind their back.
—Anonymous

If we choose personal gain at the expense of a relationship or we pass on confidential information that was shared with us privately, we would be wise to re-examine our level of integrity. If we speak about the need to treat people with respect but contradictorily belittle others, our integrity in relationships could well come into question.

Relating inconsistently to others provides excellent insight into our level of integrity. If we're abusive, threatening and manipulative, it's unlikely we will be attracting anyone to connect with us in a genuine manner. If we have the best interests of others at heart, it is more likely they will be responsive to us in our leadership capacity.

ii. Finances

The second critical area of integrity is finances. Almost everyone feels a degree of financial pressure at some time or other; in such an environment our integrity regarding finances can be tested. The ability to quickly improve our financial position, by even just slightly bending the rules, can potentially allow us to avoid some monetary pain or to make a profit. However, the ability to act with honesty, give the correct change, accept a fair trade and provide accurate financial records, even if it means forfeiting some profit, is a key indicator of our integrity.

Chapter One – Integrity

Withholding information from the tax department, submitting a false receipt, even deciding not to pay a bill may provide us with a few extra dollars, but are we winning in the area of financial integrity by doing so?

In the 1970s Tennessee Governor Ray Blanton accepted bribes in exchange for pardoning criminals; in 1868 William Tweed became a member of the New York Senate. He arranged for contractors working for the city to charge up to a hundred times the true value of the work, then shared the profits with those in on the scheme, ultimately stealing upwards of $200 million from New York taxpayers, and in 2002 China's State Food and Drug Administration head took bribes in exchange for allowing companies to register products that didn't meet safety requirements.[5]

If we engage in these self-interested practices, once they are uncovered, it will inevitably result in a loss of trust.

In private life, financial accountability is critical to the marriage relationship. Honestly declaring what we make and spend weekly, agreeing to stick to a budget (or owning up when we don't), and keeping hands off the savings account (barring an emergency) exemplify essential aspects of financial integrity between spouses. Thus, creating an environment of stability and modelling those principles to the next generation.

In business and free enterprise, being a shrewd financial operator is a healthy and wise skill to pursue. But when we are always looking to short-change whoever we're dealing with, take more than we give, promise one thing but deliver another or take advantage of a situation at someone else's expense, we're clearly lacking financial integrity.

Even if this pays off in the short term, it's not the path toward building long-term partnerships, trade associations, a good reputation or the ability to attract and influence followers.

The trail left behind with a 'win at all costs' mentality is simultaneously producing a trail of 'losers' who will not be quick to trust our integrity the next time or provide a positive referral for our reputation.

When we become known for valuing honesty and integrity over a quick dollar, we carry more weight than someone willing to compromise to get ahead financially.

A good name is more desirable than great riches;
to be esteemed is better than silver or gold.
—Proverbs 22:1

The Outworking of Integrity

The demonstration of personal integrity in our own lives and dealings with others is the first level of this integrity characteristic. The next level, however, is when we begin to apply our standards of integrity to the environment around us.

One of the measures of our level of integrity is how much tolerance we have regarding issues, practices or norms operating around us that are inconsistent with our own values, standards and beliefs.

As leaders of integrity, if we notice inconsistent behaviour around a value, concept or standard important to us within our sphere of influence, we attempt to address that inconsistency. We will not walk past the situation when it is at odds with the standard we personally hold or have publicly promoted.

We feel compelled to address the inconsistency between our

standards and the state of the environment around us.

This compulsion does not mean being aggressive or domineering, or that we try to impose our values intolerantly. Instead, we are proactive in highlighting the issue, initiating the discussion, promoting our values and seeking to bring change where we see something out of alignment.

In other words, . . . we do something!

> *Leadership is an action, not a position.*
> —Donald McGannon

If we simply ignore or tolerate behaviour that does not agree with the standard we hold up, it can reflect our level of integrity.

Craig was the CEO of a medium-sized organisation and for the last eighteen months had been selling the message of 'accountable behaviours'—his company's new mantra. That is, completing actions when you said, or when required, to ensure the organisation kept ticking like clockwork.

Morning teas, staff introductions and farewells, annual staff days and corporate newsletters were filled with the message of 'accountable behaviours'. However, it was commonly known throughout all levels of the company that in five of the six direct reports to Craig, the senior managers, never met the due date to complete their tasks. Amongst lower-level staffers affected by the unmet deadlines of their superiors, this was a frequent discussion point. And yet there were no consequences. Craig did nothing. Nevertheless, the message to finish tasks on time continued.

As you can imagine, Craig's message of accountable actions was completely undermined. Staffers saw his message as simply 'all talk and no action' and secretly joked about it as a farcical part of their business culture.

When this happens, the message the leader is sending is that there are two standards: the one everyone else is expected to abide by and the one he and the corporate bosses follow as it suits them.

By tolerating a standard that is inconsistent with what we are espousing, we demonstrate a lack of integrity that undermines the culture of our leadership and the genuineness of our character. It tells people that our values are a 'nice idea' but not ones we hold any real allegiance to or are prepared to enforce.

The test of our integrity

Our willingness and determination to confront and address issues that do not align with our stated standards or values in an appropriate and people-focused way, can eventually be the *defining test of our integrity*. There is a definite point in time where our leadership integrity is demonstrated by our decision to move from talking to acting.

We either act to bring about positive change, or we shy away from the problem and simply reinforce the status quo.

Without this willingness to act, there is no potential to reshape the environment, align people to a vision, reset cultural standards, or change unproductive or negative dynamics in the situation around us. We are destined to accept the values and standard others set for our team, community, or society.

What you allow, is what will continue.
—Anonymous

Integrity Leadership in the Community

A willingness to take action to support personal values can also be demonstrated by leadership in the community—for example, through politics.

Stephen was an elected state member of parliament in his city-based constituency. One of the issues that had recently inflamed his community was the pro-life versus pro-choice debate, and both sides were pressuring him to make his stance public. Rather than refer to his own convictions, or even party policy, Stephen referred to the popularity polls. 'Analyse the focus groups', he told his advisors. 'I'm going to support whatever side creates the least conflict for my office, is supported by the media and helps me get re-elected in eighteen months'.

But if we operate according to our internal conviction of principles, we feel compelled to take action to support our values, not our popularity or job security.

The action to support our values can be seemingly small steps. It can take the form of calling a meeting to discuss the issue, supporting a political party that aligns with our values, starting a petition to engage community support, developing a community lobby group or becoming a voice on the issue via different media forums.

When we take on this role, we are prepared to step out of our comfort zone of anonymity and into the potential glare of the public square—and possibly endure potential negative feedback. Our motivating energy is on supporting, defending and promoting the value we hold dear. This motivation provides us with the courage to override the internal fear and anxiety associated with taking this step and speaking out. Our integrity to act on our beliefs that we consider 'non negotiables' may even create tension within existing relationships of friends and family, politicians, decision-makers or other groups as a result of promoting the value we believe in.

Integrity Leadership in Teams

In a team or group environment, whether a family, workgroup or community network, if we as the leader, the standard-bearer, fail to oversee and uphold the values and culture in the group, it is prone to descend into a melee of confusion.

When members know that no standard exists or is being maintained, that their behaviour has no consequences and that no one is holding them accountable, a common pattern emerges. Without an active integrity leader in the group, then typically the most dominant personality or the comfort and convenience of the majority becomes the prevailing force.

The lunchroom walls of a high-quality custom steel-fabrication workshop were adorned with posters displaying mandatory workplace legislative information. This included occupational health and safety requirements, first-aid contacts and the incident-reporting process. However, there was a disconnect between the group culture and the messages in the posters, as illustrated below:

- hanging in front of the Hard Hats Are Compulsory safety sign were four of the workshop's five staff helmets.

- the first aid-officer's contact details were covered by a picture of the boat he was selling.

- and someone had creatively written under the company value of 'I Will Avoid Injury'... *'then don't tell me how to do my job'*.

Not surprisingly, this workshop typically operated with a recklessness regarding safety protocols that in the last eighteen months resulted in three severe incidents, one requiring hospitalisation of their staff. Without a standard bearer, the group had slipped into what behaviour was the most convenient.

By not addressing inconsistencies with their stated values and not creating accountability, the company leaders were forced to live with what others decided the standards should be.

As leaders, our silence on issues relating to the integrity of our culture and values will always have a price.

Control your own destiny or someone else will.
—Jack Welch

If a builder let his team of contractors build a house according to whatever standards each of them felt were suitable, the house would end up an incohesive mishmash of plans, designs and qualities based on every contributor's personal preference—rendering it unrecognisable and unusable. If the builder were not prepared to ensure his particular preferences were applied and his standards upheld across the entire build process, how could he promise a product of a certain quality to the clients? He could not.

When we don't develop integrity to the point where we are willing to take action to promote, enforce and defend it, we are not fulfilling an essential leadership role of setting and maintaining standards. By doing so, it leaves us, and those connected to us, vulnerable to self-appointed leaders filling the void.

Recognising and Responding to Competing Values

When someone or something in our team is not consistent with our values, and we are a leader of integrity, it instantly creates a tension in the environment that demands our response. This situation effectively issues a challenge to the culture we are building, and to us as the responsible gatekeeper, that says, 'Either you will change me, or I'll change you'.

If the issue is not addressed, we will be forced to accept this alternate value, thus accepting the compromise it brings to what we are building because our tolerance normalises that value as part of our culture.

Governing the Cultural Integrity

To the uninformed, a small termite could not possibly present any danger to the integrity of an immense building structure. But to the wise builder, a single termite can represent the potential presence of a colony of destructive agents that will ultimately undermine the foundations and the functionality of the building.

A minor issue an individual has relating to our standards may be just that. But it might also represent a significant underlying tone, attitude or agenda that, left unchecked, can establish a potentially destructive dynamic that will contaminate the environment.

Lily managed a small government-funded health service with around twenty staff. Students and recent graduates often joined the team, as there was always work to do in the under-resourced service, and this way it came at a minimal cost.

Lily noticed that in recent months Joanne was making a special effort to spend time with the new employees and graduates, who were having lunches as a group. Every now and then she overheard a comment tainted with a hint of sarcasm or disapproval on issues those in the group weren't involved in or shouldn't have known about, which she found odd. Having unsuccessfully applied to be the manager several times, Joanne had not taken the disappointment well, still harbouring bitterness about someone else being in 'her' role.

Lily began to suspect that Joanne was recruiting new staff to 'her' team.

Sensing the potential damage if allowed to continue, she called Joanne in. Explaining that she was always happy to receive feedback, she reemphasized to Joanne the invitation to speak to her directly if she felt strongly about any issues. At the next two sitewide team meetings she spoke to everyone about the need for honest communication and feedback, highlighting how disappointed she would be, for example, if people had thoughts on the health service, sharing them with others but not her. A topic that resulted in several eyes looking at their shoes and some red cheeks.

A month later, in the staff newsletter, she wrote about the importance of working together, then implemented a new program that assigned formal 'buddies' for new recruits so that Joanne did not become their pseudo contact point. Over the next few months the group lunches Joanne arranged slowly dissipated, new staff and graduates were connecting well to engaged, productive members across the workforce, and a much more positive tone was re-established in the atmosphere.

If we let issues slip for too long, the task of reclaiming the territory, re-establishing standards, realigning practices and resetting culture is then a large one and has to come, potentially, at considerable cost and casualties. The more a counterculture is allowed to get established and embedded, both in individuals and in the team, the harder the task of removing it.

While the tip of the iceberg is visible to the captain of the ship, the more considerable concern is always what's hidden under the surface. Captains have to be scanning, investigating and interpreting what is seen to assess what is unseen, and take appropriate action in response to the danger it presents.

Spending time to 'look and see' is an integral part of identifying dangers to our 'ship', whether that's our family, workplace or community. A conversation that addresses a small reaction we notice today can save us from facing a mutiny a year away.

Will and Tess kept a very close eye on their ten-year-old daughter Zoe's attitude—quick to identify and address signs of disrespect from Zoe toward them as parents, her schoolteachers or even sports coaches or other authority figures. Setting the bar high, they diligently maintained an 'attitude-free home', as they termed it. Why?

With Zoey's older sister Cara, now eighteen, Will and Tess had taken a very different approach. When Cara was eight, she started making comments about her 'stupid teachers' and the 'dumb home rules'. They glossed over the comments, excusing her: 'She's just a kid blowing off some steam', they told themselves. Cara's attitude, however, left unaddressed, continued to escalate and had now taken hold in her as a permanent, defining pattern of behaviour. This led her down a dangerous path of refusing to comply with basic home or societal protocols. She dropped out of high school, left home at her parents' request due to her constant insults and abuse of trust, and was living on welfare, unable to work for any of those 'idiot bosses'.

They were determined not to use the same laissez-faire approach with their younger child. Instead, they committed to being diligent in addressing unhealthy attitudes they saw in her as they came up.

'I know I'm the boss on the org chart', Paul, a grocery-warehouse despatch centre supervisor said defeatedly, 'but the guys really run the place. I lost the ability to enforce standards or targets about three years ago, when a couple of them refused to comply with new rules. It's just easier to let them do what they like now. And saves all the conflict and stress'.

Paul was fired when his new boss asked why his team hadn't met the outputs for the month. Paul explained that he didn't really set the targets, as the guys in his team 'just like to work at their own pace'.

The company judged Paul as being completely negligent in his leadership task of aligning staff to company expectations. Paul's old boss had been let go because he had never created accountability or provided support for Paul to take action and lead his team.

Avoiding the issue never resolves it and doesn't make us any safer. Paul suffered the consequences.

He and his old boss failed to understand that if we don't proactively address these types of issues, they will fester and grow, and at some stage, they will land back on our doorstep.

Influencing Factors That Prevent Leaders from Addressing Issues

Our inability or unwillingness to demonstrate integrity at this level, confronting and address issues not aligned to our values, can be related to several factors:

i. **Fear of conflict**

Conflict is a naturally difficult area for most of us, and consequently, most of us tend to avoid it wherever we can.

We have to understand, though, that leadership always involves an element of conflict. Conflict is not only necessary but constructive and healthy if we handle it in the right way.

The idea of disturbing comfortable, familiar relationships by introducing a discussion topic or new initiative that may create conflict can be a daunting prospect. The fear of upsetting these relationships, the potential adverse reaction, the possible loss of popularity and the possibility of offence being taken by the other party toward us can be enough to stop us from raising the issue at all.

As leaders of integrity, we can never allow personal relationships to take priority over the mandate we are entrusted with, whether in our family, workplace, or community. We must apply the same standards to everyone. *Relationships serve the vision, not vice versa.*

We may have a lot of nice, friendly relationships with our team members at work, which creates a very comfortable environment. But these relationships can be devoid of any truth, purpose, accountability or challenge. In that case, the situation ultimately reduces the effectiveness and unity of the team, because we built a culture based on convenience, comfort and mutual nondisclosure rather than the purpose and values we want to capture and pursue.

We must be led by what the right thing to do is. If we open a discussion with someone about an issue that is having a detrimental effect on the group, as sensitively and with as much care as we can, but we still receive a hostile, adverse reaction, we've still done the right thing.

Steve was the manager of a local municipality leisure department, which consisted of 8 pools and 3 indoor sports courts. Steve's second in charge, Rachel, was responsible for co-ordinating all the staff rosters. She was a large, boisterous, blunt woman who had been in the role as long as Steve, 15 years. She bullied her staff, making them take shifts they didn't ask for, was rude to them when communicating and would often cut their hours completely if they showed any sign of resistance to her domineering approach.

Steve had received numerous complaints from team members, but as one long term casual described 'He doesn't have the guts to stand up to Rachel and pull her into line. He'd rather just ignore it, so he stays away and we are all left to live with her'.

As integrity leaders, we don't sweep things under the carpet, and we don't hope problems just disappear. This behaviour does not meet the expectation of those who are relying on us to stand up, speak up and create order and boundaries in the environment they are living and working in.

ii. Self-focus

As we grow into leaders of integrity, we realise we have a duty to care for the behaviour, performance and welfare of all those connected with us, not just our own.

We realise that ultimately it is the team's performance that counts.

If we lose sight of this, we can quickly become the 'best player on the worst team'. If we think we're performing well, but none of our group is, the truth is ... we're not performing well, as a leader.

When we have empowered our group, equipped them to succeed, created accountability and support to enable everyone's success—when the group is achieving team-focused results, feels valued and inspired, and when we are addressing the attitudes and behaviours in others that jeopardise team success—that's when we can say we're winning as leaders.

If we are a high-performing, high-achieving person carrying excellent standards of personal integrity, but take no interest in developing and reproducing this culture in people or processes around us, it demonstrates we have not yet moved into the next dimension of leadership integrity.

iii. Level of internal belief

When we carry a strong internal belief about a value or standard, we are prepared to, figuratively speaking, 'go to war' over it. If it's only a nice idea to us, or a politically correct value we support in theory but don't wholeheartedly believe in, it's unlikely we will take action to address anyone or anything that is carrying a competing philosophy. The gap between the action we take and the values we stand for represents our quality as a leader.

Carrying Integrity in Our Lives

If we cannot carry integrity of character, it limits our ability to lead effectively.

When integrity has been well formed in our lives, our values are clear, our character is proven, and we are prepared to defend and promote these standards with people on our teams and the broader community.

We have demonstrated consistency of character over a period of time and a range of situations, and those connected to us have a strong sense of who we are, and what we stand for, allowing them to make a commitment to us knowing that 'what they see, is what they get'.

CHAPTER TWO

Conviction of Purpose

Conviction: The quality of showing that one is firmly convinced of what one believes or says
Purpose: The reason for which something is done or created, or for which something exists

What on earth are we here for? What's our role and function during our time on the planet?

These potentially challenging questions are important to explore to assist our leadership development.

When we move towards becoming leaders strongly convinced about our purpose, we begin to develop a deep, internal, fixed belief about the role we are called to fulfil. This understanding may involve a group, our family, an organisation or a community. The role may lie anywhere between one specific action at a certain moment in history, to a progressively unfolding, recurring theme of activity that we develop throughout our lifetime.

Our conviction of purpose grows as our belief in it is internalised. This purpose becomes our own intrinsic 'assignment' that describes what we feel is our leadership call.

An 'assignment' that parents might take on in the family domain is to raise kids with a strong character and values. In business, it's the entrepreneur wanting to birth a product, turn around a company or create wealth to pass on to the next generation. In the community setting it may be to successfully establish a literacy program. Or in the workplace it could be the determined school principal who makes sure to keep the curriculum headed in a certain direction. For individuals it may be as specific as breaking through their fear and overcoming limitations in their life.

Our assignment can be whatever applies to us at a point in time in a specific situation. *It's the particular mountain we've chosen to, or need to, climb to move forward.* We volunteer for our assignment by our internal conviction; it is not imposed on us by somebody else, like a paid job.

While our sense of assignment may well be endorsed by others, who validate it, ultimately, we reach the point where we believe it, even when others don't. This conviction starts to become real on the inside the moment we choose to believe it.

The mystery of human existence lies not in just staying alive, but in finding something to live for.
—Fyodor Dostoyevsky

Dr. Bronwyn King worked in the lung-cancer department of a major metropolitan hospital specialising in oncology. She had witnessed the horrors of the effects of lung cancer caused by tobacco use that kills around six million people a year, despite the fact that media outlets have grown 'weary' of reporting on it.

Coincidentally, she and her husband Mark were buying a house, which prompted an investment conversation with a representative

Chapter Two – Conviction of Purpose

from her superannuation fund. In the hospital cafeteria, almost as an afterthought, King asked him if she was to specify how she wanted her money invested. Her adviser explained there was no need, as it was in 'the default option', just like with 75 per cent of the population. 'Or there's the 'greenie' option that doesn't involve investment in tobacco, alcohol or mining?'

Stunned that she, like many of her colleagues, was investing in the promotion of tobacco sales, she felt a deep burden to *do* something. This sense of assignment spurred her into a mission. Knowing nothing about the world of investment, but being very clear in her purpose, she established Tobacco Free Portfolios, a not-for-profit organisation that aims to eliminate tobacco from investment portfolios globally.

The organisation has since created tobacco-free finance policies implemented by over forty Australian superannuation funds (including King's original superfund) and by financial organisations across ten countries, diverting more than *AU $20 billion away from investment in tobacco*. For distinguished service to community health, Bronwyn was awarded the Order of Australia (AO) in 2019.

'Early on, many colleagues thought it was silly and that I was being distracted from the "real" work of research. I was told to reconsider what I was doing and that I was making a terrible mistake', Bronwyn recalled about the start of her journey. 'But it was just so fascinating to me that I found I couldn't stop'.[6]

If we're going to be leaders, we must have a purpose we are convinced of. Otherwise, we will typically resort to a default pseudo-leadership approach—merely trying to satisfy the majority, fit in with popular opinion and take the most comfortable path available to avoid discomfort. In this void created by a lack of connection to a higher purpose, our top priority may revolve merely around maintaining the status quo. When we reach this point, we are just administrating.

Even if we are self-serving in our outlook, we can still carry a measure of purpose. However, the purpose we develop the strongest convictions about will involve the success, development and benefit of others, not just ourselves.

When we combine a strong sense of purpose with a conviction to pursue that purpose, we acquire a clear intrinsic mandate. This combination sets us on a course and propels us forward, driving our action and fuelling our energy levels as we lock onto the completion of our assignment.

It's the repetition of affirmations that leads to belief.
And once that belief becomes a deep conviction,
things begin to happen.
—Muhammad Ali

Measuring Conviction

The depth of our convictions is measured through our actions. Sometimes we can unexpectedly find ourselves in emergency situations that require split-second decisions. At other times, we demonstrate our conviction daily as we continually work towards a particular goal.

Either way, we can't fake conviction. When the rubber hits the road, it's the invisible, inner belief we hold that manifests into the visible actions we take.

With a deep sense of conviction, we are prepared to pursue our assignment, even if it takes us out of a place of comfort and into a place of potential pain and unrest. Our intent to stand for what we believe is *right* may lead us to experience a range of negative consequences, such as public criticism, opposition, personal loss and loss of popularity with the majority.

If we don't have this sense of purpose, we will never step out of the comfort zone, as we only have everything to lose. But when we do, we also see everything we have to gain.

Joanne was terrified of public speaking but had a strong belief in her message about supporting people with depression in her community. Despite her fear, she started speaking in schools, businesses and senior-citizen organisations, informing them about support groups, help lines and where to find resources. By overcoming her fear, she defeated this obstacle standing in the way of the purpose she felt called to pursue. 'I still feel ill before I speak in public'. Joanne laughs. 'But that doesn't stop me. I know it's what I'm here to do'.

As we foster this force within us, it becomes more substantial than the limiting power of the barriers that hold us. We move from being controlled by our fear to being led by our convictions.

This process of breaking through our internal boundaries creates a dynamic that, when repeated, sets up a pattern of being able to meet new obstacles as they arise. We develop the ability to progressively walk towards our vision of who and what we are called to become.

As purpose-driven leaders, we are *sold out* to our cause and set a standard of commitment that acts as a benchmark for those who come to join us.

Leadership: Convicted v. Convenient

The other end of the spectrum to leadership that operates by a deep conviction of purpose is leadership based on convenience.

This approach is where we are happy to fill a role or assume a title, as long as it provides some personal benefits such as an attractive salary, free product or services, or a healthy dose of prestige.

When we function out of the realm of convenience, we are less driven by any sense of conviction or purpose, and more focused on keeping the status quo of the environment that provides us with the benefits we enjoy.

The Life-Shaping Power of Purpose

When the conviction of our purpose begins to grow in our heart, it starts to influence our behaviour and reshape our life.

Like an anchor point we can fix ourselves to, our mission becomes an increasingly more potent motivating force pulling us forward, past the limiting dynamics and circumstances holding us back.

> *If you have a strong purpose in life, you don't have to be pushed. Your passion will drive you there.*
> —Roy T. Bennett

Whether a clarity of purpose occurs instantaneously (or more likely over time), it simultaneously begins to burn a conviction in our heart with a life-changing impact.

Tim grew up in a rough neighbourhood without a place to call home, surviving by stealing cars in a gang. His teenage life had little going for it, except that one day turning up unannounced to try out for the high-school basketball team, he was noticed. Without any previous coaching, not even in proper sports shoes, Tim still stood out, with his incredible athleticism and fierce

Chapter Two – Conviction of Purpose

competitiveness—ultimately earning a spot on the team, ironically for a school he rarely attended.

His coach soon learned that he was unruly, ill disciplined, had a habit of resorting to fighting his way out of pressure situations and was a constant source of frustration. Yet he was also an unstoppable force, with his six-foot-five frame, speed, power and quickly improving skills. Despite his wild temperament, he earnt a scholarship to college, where he broke all-time scoring records. At the end of his college career he was in discussions for an NBA contract in the elite American league.

But along his journey, Tim experienced a spiritual awakening. During this final year, he felt a calling to serve in a Christian basketball ministry overseas. In answer to the perplexed questioning—why did he give up the chance of a lifetime to play in the 'big time'?—he explained, 'I always knew what I was good at, but I never knew what the purpose of that talent was until now'.

A long way from the lights and glamour of elite sports, Tim instead led over 1,100 short-term touring mission teams on exhibition games in the cities and provinces, playing in palaces, prisons, universities, military bases and leper colonies—all the while building connections with local churches and in the process distributing over 600,000 Bible study courses.

Sometimes the most obvious pathway in life is not the one we ultimately find our purpose in.

The two most important days in your life are the day you are born and the day you find out why.
—Mark Twain

This growing sense of purpose accelerates our leadership capacity.

When the conviction of our mission grows, it becomes the primary shaping influence on us, and we learn to eliminate and break through our excuses for not fulfilling the purpose we feel called to perform. It energises us, overriding and overpowering potentially competing forces that may stop us, such as our culture, our past experience, previous failures or our fears.

Without this, we stay stuck behind the limitations that our internal dynamics tell us is the boundary of our life's purpose, and therefore the boundary of our leadership.

Purpose and Priorities

Our level of conviction of purpose will often be seen in our choice of priorities. For example, a father who has a deep conviction to protect and defend his son will prioritise his child's life over his own and willingly put himself at risk to ensure his child's survival.

A person who is convinced that her purpose is to connect with and help people at a community level to develop their education and life skills may prioritise working in a community-oriented role rather than an alternative corporate position devoid of community involvement, even if it pays a higher salary.

The degree that our priorities align with our purpose indicates the degree our purpose has impacted our life. If we believe our mission involves writing new computer programs but only spend an hour every few months developing them, there is a disconnect between our purpose and priorities.

Your priorities aren't what you say they are.
They are revealed by how you live.
—Unknown

Chapter Two – Conviction of Purpose

Tanya was the coordinator of the local Neighbourhood House, a non-profit community-based hub designed to offer opportunities to learn new skills, stay involved in favourite activities and make connections in the community.

At the House, the facilities were basic and generally needed maintenance, evidenced by the peeling white paint of the front weatherboard porch. Staffing was minimal (Tanya was the only paid member), and equipment such as cutlery and crockery, printers and computers frequently consisted of hand-me-downs and donations.

Yet six days a week the House was abuzz with the rattle and hum of men and women—young and old—participating in programs, outings and social groups. A range of personalities met, mixed and shared laughs, tears, friendships and life together. Tanya earned a minimum wage, worked double the hours she was paid for, performed tasks well outside her Position Description qualifications and was constantly facilitating events, logistics and people during and after designated hours. Without her additional 'elbow grease', the House would clearly run at a reduced capacity.

It surprised me to learn that years ago, upon graduating from university, Tanya embarked down a very different, well-paying career path. Intrigued, I had to ask, 'Tanya, why did you not go down that path? How did you end up in this role?'

She told me it came about by chance initially—when she helped a relative at another Neighbourhood House. 'I realised that my career was all about me, and all my friends were living that life, whereas this role was all about others. And I began to develop a belief that I wanted to use my talents and energy to make a difference in the lives of other people as much as I could, for as long as I could'.

The realisation of purpose in Tanya's life showed itself in a change of course. Tanya's internal motivation overrode all external priorities. Tanya stands out as a leader of conviction about her life purpose.

Where there is no sense of internal purpose, we will be led by external motivators and invariably end up following the *best offer* (as it appears on paper) to meet our personal needs. These external motivators are usually measured by material items, such as money, position, titles or possessions—not always the best indicators to measure how accurately we are fulfilling our purpose.

When we transition to becoming leaders of purpose, however, we are not led by external rewards, no matter what the offer. We have reoriented our priorities to measure our success by how we are fulfilling our purpose, not external trappings and quantity of possessions.

Purpose and Change

As our sense of purpose develops inside us, it grows to the point where it creates a desire to improve something in our environment. We feel a burden and an angst to take action to address whatever is blocking our purpose, and we are increasingly unable to tolerate the current situation.

Discontent is the first necessity of progress.
—Thomas Edison

These two elements, *change* and *purpose*, often work together. As it grows inside us, this *change energy* cannot be contained. Eventually, it pours out of us, creating a tension with the existing

Chapter Two – Conviction of Purpose

environment we feel called to influence.

This situation increases the potential for a *cultural clash*. The visible or invisible structures in the environment that maintain the current conditions exert a natural resistance to change, and therefore there is a reaction against our attempts to introduce it. The established forces conspire to maintain the status quo.

As leaders of purpose and conviction, we can meet this resistance, exerting force against it so that over a period of time, our sustained efforts can break through.

If we carry a low level of conviction, it is unlikely we will even feel the need to change anything around us. But even if we wanted to, it is unlikely we will have enough *horsepower* to sustain our effort.

If our leadership only revolves around a title, we can say the right things and present a polished image but carry no ability to shift anything in the environment. The status quo is under no threat from well-groomed position-based leaders with superficial convictions.

Purpose and Persecution

Our conviction can often be measured by our willingness to face and endure persecution, usually administered by the gatekeepers of the status quo.

Australian Nancy Bird was just four years old in 1919 when she set her heart on becoming a pilot, eagerly jumping on and off the back fence of her home imitating a flying machine, playing what she labelled the 'epiplane' game in her earnest attempt to say 'aeroplane'.

At the age of nineteen, after two years of weekly lessons, she reached her goal in 1935 by gaining her commercial pilot's license. However, opposition to Nancy as a female pilot grew; she endured constant opposition from male colleagues and politicians over several years that built enough pressure to actually force Bird to stop flying. Her beloved Gypsy Moth plane was even sold for target practice as part of World War II training drills.

Despite the concerted campaign to keep her grounded, Nancy knew her destiny in life was to be flying in the clouds. She persevered with undwindling passion until she eventually flew again after the war, creating the Australian Women's Pilots Association in the process and leading the charge for the Royal Australian Air Force to set up the women's division. Nancy was presented with an OBE in 1966 by the Queen herself and was forever known as 'The Angel of the Outback'.[7]

By taking an opposing view to mainstream public opinion, we may experience community backlash. But being prepared to live out of our conviction that opposes the mainstream norm is a strong indicator we are following our purpose.

When the whole world is silent, even one voice becomes powerful.
—Malala Yousafzai

Malala Yousafzai, a Pakistani girl, was just seventeen, when in 2014 she became the youngest person ever awarded the Nobel Peace Prize. When she was only eleven, the Taliban seized control of her town, and the extremists prohibited girls from attending the local school. Having a deep love for education, she spoke out publicly against this oppressive order on behalf of all girls at her school, staunchly defending their right to learn. Her stance made her a Taliban target, and in October 2012 she was attacked and shot in the head, but amazingly awoke ten days later in an English hospital.

Once recovered, she again fought for the rights of girls to access education. Her organisation, The Malala Fund, invests internationally in developing educators and activists to create a world where all girls can learn and lead. Today she travels all over the world to help girls fight poverty, wars, child marriage and gender discrimination preventing them from going to school.[8]

If we are prepared to state our case or act only when it is deemed popular or acceptable, or when it doesn't cost us anything, we are being led more by our comfort than our conviction, not yet having developed a deep belief about our purpose. When we are prepared to endure loss, pain and criticism as a result of our beliefs, we know we are carrying a conviction.

Nothing will divert me from my purpose.
—Abraham Lincoln

Purpose and Longevity

Some people hold leadership roles for short periods or in a specific event, then move on. With a deep conviction of purpose, however, we may dedicate significant portions of our life, even decades, to the same cause. We do this because we do not see our involvement as a burden or as something to do until we get a better offer but feel called to it as long as we are on the earth.

When we reach this level of conviction, the concept of *other opportunities* holds no attraction to us. The only opportunity of interest is to fulfil our mission. All other opportunities, activities, offers and obligations take a back seat to this consuming quest;

hence, we typically find very extended tenures of conviction-based leaders. When we operate at this level, we carry the mindset that asks, 'If I didn't do this, what else would I do?'

Purpose and Legacy

Sometimes this conviction is transferred to willing followers and can span generations. Our mission as a leader does not always have to be new; it may well be the continuation of a forefather's vision that we take on board as our own.

That's why often we become the greatest leader we can be by becoming the greatest follower, as we can capture an existing purpose from a preceding generation and continue it into the future.

Key Indicators We Are Leading with a Conviction of Purpose

i. We carry a strong momentum and energy
   The arrow shot from the archer's bow is *driven with force* accurately towards its target. So too are we as the purpose-driven leader. Either through the process of time or by sudden revelation, we become internally convinced about the role we are called to perform and are set on course. We may not always know how we will get there, but a momentum and energy within us is propelling us to reach our destination with purpose.

Purpose provides activation energy for living.
—Mihaly Csikszentmihalyi

Chapter Two – Conviction of Purpose

ii. **We are motivated by purpose, not by external rewards or recognition**

While popularity polls, success and the personal benefits of holding positions of influence fuel a particular type of leader, as we saw in the example of Tanya, who chose to coordinate the neighbourhood house, as purpose-filled leaders we are driven primarily by an internal conviction. Nothing is more appealing or motivating to us than the fulfilment of our life's assignment.

iii. **We take responsibility**

As leaders with a conviction of purpose, we carry a burden of personal responsibility for our cause. We are not prepared to say, 'It's someone else's job'. Instead, we proactively volunteer to be part of the solution, before being asked. We don't need to determine whether taking action is listed in our Position Description, because we're not led by the legalistic fine print of an employment agreement. Nor do we need to conduct a cost/benefit analysis. If we're already internally convinced about our need to be part of the solution, we will take responsibility, and then take action.

iv. **We stay the course**

If this conviction of purpose is not formed well in us, when failure or external pressure works against us, we may be tempted to opt out of the contest—quitting if the journey gets tough or jumping ship if we get a better offer. If our belief or our stance starts to cost us some reputation, finances or security, we are susceptible to giving up.

Success, surprisingly, can also derail our pursuit of purpose, as we may potentially become satisfied when we only have half the job done, having attained some of our goals or made some progress toward our end goal.

To have success, you can't let failure stop you.
To have great success, you can't let success stop you.
—Robert Brault

To a truly convicted leader of purpose, the idea of giving up in the face of adversity, or after we have achieved only a measure of success, is not an option. We may even hold this attitude in the face of logical or rational evidence that says it's reasonable to stop or give up, but we will stay the course no matter the opposition or the outcome.

Galileo, now referred to as the 'father of modern science', faced the wrath of the Catholic Church when he advocated the Copernican view that the earth revolved around the sun, and not vice versa. In 1633 he was summoned to the Roman Inquisition and convicted of 'vehement suspicion of heresy'. He was threatened with torture and placed under house arrest for the rest of his life. Yet he held fast to his theory, burdened to bring this truth to the world, and continued to develop further scientific papers, since proven factual, even while under arrest. In the twentieth century Popes Pius XII and John Paul II made formal statements of regret for how the church treated him.

Engaging with Purpose

The roles we perform in our daily life may be the source we derive our predominant sense of purpose from. For example, being a member of the family unit (we're a daughter, a mother and a sister), having a job (we're a cleaner) and participating in our activities and groups (we're a member of the Wednesday-night tennis competition).

These are all productive, worthy, healthy pursuits—vital ingredients to a well-functioning family and society. The act of dedicated parenting in itself changes the world of that child.

However, we can also engage with purpose on a level that has an added dimension. We can still place importance on our family welfare, our vocation and/or our social activities, while also recognising the inner call to a purpose that extends beyond these boundaries. We may begin to feel a call to a broader issue, which affects perhaps as well our network of family and friends, our community, region or even nation.

We may not have any experience, skills or resources—or even a plan—to bring anything of what we are feeling into effect, but we begin to foster the idea that our purpose is connected to something bigger. When we start to touch this dimension of higher purpose, we begin to see the needs of all the people potentially affected by it. Our view of our everyday activities, such as our job, also begins to shift.

We start to realize that our job is not necessarily our purpose. It may be how we pay the bills or what we're skilled in but doesn't necessarily define what we are called to do or who we are called to be.

If we have connected to a purpose transcending our immediate network, job, family or circumstances, it begins to draw us upward to see a bigger picture—on a larger scale.

For example, while one person idly casts a political vote, another, with a deeper conviction, may run as a candidate, support a campaign or be an influencer through public debate. The latter may even take time off work and invest money and energy to promote an outcome.

The thing that distinguishes these responses is their level of conviction in the matter.

In 1980, Candy Lightner's thirteen-year-old daughter was run over and killed in California by a drunken driver with numerous previous drink-driving offences. He had been arrested by police at an earlier hit-and-run incident just the week prior. Despite having no experience or interest in social reform or politics, and by her own admission having never even seen the need to register to vote, Candy was determined to change societal attitudes about the low-level consequences and lax laws around drink driving to prevent further tragedies such as she had experienced. She quit her job, and from the humble beginnings of her kitchen table she established Mothers Against Drunk Driving (MADD). She visited the Californian governor's office every day to advance her cause until the governor launched a state commission on drunk driving, followed in 1984 by US President Ronald Regan appointing her to the National Commission Against Drunk Driving. MADD successfully lobbied for national legislation changes to drink-driving laws and has grown to six hundred chapters across the globe, with three million members and supporters in America alone. It is now one of the country's most influential non-profit organisations and has helped to cut drink-driving fatalities by half.[9]

Candy's sense of purpose was redefined and expanded from a local to a national perspective.

When you walk in purpose you collide with destiny.
—Ralph Buchanan

Relationship, Connections and Purpose

The pursuit and achievement of purpose is rarely a solo activity.

There are specific connections that we must build to help unwrap and fulfil the area of purpose in our life:

i. Peers

We can connect with others to mutually support our pursuit of purpose—not in a competitive manner but by supplying and receiving support, camaraderie and inspiration.

When we are clear on our purpose, we can partner with the right people, who are similarly aligned to the frequency we are tuned in to.

We can distinguish, then between those connections that revolve around purpose and those that may be more like acquaintances.

ii. Apprentices

These are the ones we are calling forth to join with us. Just as we are receiving from others to take us higher, we are imparting to apprentices to equip them to progress on our shared journey into purpose.

iii. Forefathers and Mentors

These people, who went before us, established a stature that enables them to mentor us, sow purpose into us and call us further into our unique role. They provide the blueprints and frameworks that gives us direction to move forward, equipping us with the resources and capacity to fulfill our purpose.

Accurate connections with these people allow us to draw from their skills, character, understanding, wisdom and passion.

- **Forefathers, purpose and followership**

The *Collins Dictionary* defines 'followership' as the ability or willingness to follow a leader.

Our purpose as a leader may well be to follow another person who has commenced an initiative or a campaign in a particular domain that we believe in. When we have connected with that person, we are inspired to build on the foundation of their work.

It is not uncommon to find that the best followers make the best leaders.

The best leaders know how and when to follow.
—Unknown

We must understand that we do not need to start our own project or activity to be a leader. To follow and support someone else's purpose does not mean we haven't found our purpose or that we are not leaders. Often the leaders who exert the most influence carry the torch of another's vision.

You cannot be a leader and ask other people to follow you, unless you know how to follow too.
—Sam Rayburn

Followership is not an indicator that we are not good enough to take the 'top job'—not a derogatory term to describe our 'second fiddle' status. Purpose is not positional, so cannot be mapped on an organisation chart, but is measured by our heart attitude and level of investment in the assignment.

Most of us will likely find our leadership roles in the area of followership, because our starting point to enter our purpose is often through supporting someone else's.

If we believe in the purpose of an existing work established by a pioneering leader, we can find our purpose by serving theirs.

> *To excel at leadership you must first master followership.*
> —Truett Cathy

True followership transcends the transactional approach of employer and employee or an association of convenience; it moves into the realm of genuine heart connection and a shared purpose.

As we commit to our followership, we begin to partner with the pioneer and leaders of the movement. Gradually emptying ourselves of our own agenda, we carry more of the pioneer's message, conviction and burden, and in so doing transition from just enjoying being part of the group, to becoming a co-labourer with the pioneer to see the pioneer's assignment progress. This helps the work to rise to even greater heights, as now at least two lives are driving the same purpose. When we see purpose as a transferable entity, it takes on a generational dynamic that ensures its fulfillment and longevity.

- **Forefathers, purpose and covering**

Whether we have taken a step to pursue a dream or follow a conviction or have simply travelled the journey of life, we all understand that we can benefit from having someone who provides us protection, wisdom and support. There are many snags, hazards, attacks and opposing forces we are likely to run up against in the pursuit of our purpose. If we have appropriate oversight, we are more likely to make it.

Forefathers or mentors who have a stature and who we have a genuine connection can potentially offer this covering.

English business magnate and founder of the Virgin Group Sir Richard Branson admits, 'If you ask any successful business person, they will always have had a great mentor at some point along the road'. He attributed his success to the practical guidance and inspiration from pioneering airline entrepreneur Sir Freddy Laker, of which Branson admits, 'We wouldn't have gotten anywhere in the airline industry without Freddie's down-to-earth wisdom'.[10]

If we are just independent, solo operators, we are more exposed to attack, susceptible to errors—over reliant on our own resources, more vulnerable to being picked off by an opposition intent on putting us out of the game.

A key prerequisite to securing covering from a forefather over our life is an ability to voluntarily become accountable to that person.

If in our life and leadership we are unable to be transparent or accountable to anyone, we increase the risk of becoming inaccurate in the pursuit of our purpose—taking others down a wayward path. As we increase our transparency to forefathers, we allow them greater access, which in turn equips us to live out our purpose. These people have our best interests at heart; they provide us with feedback on our progress, performance and approach. They validate our ability to progress, equip us to overcome obstacles, guide our decision-making, counsel us where we are wrong and prevent us from self-inflicted disasters.

Chapter Two –Conviction of Purpose

Every son quotes his father in words and deeds.
—Unknown

CHAPTER THREE

Vision

Vision: A mental image of what the future will or could be like
The faculty or state of being able to see

Vision is the ability to see far to what is not yet revealed (foresight) and to accurately see into the truth of a situation (insight).

> *Vision is the art of seeing what is invisible to others.*
> —Jonathan Swift

A defining factor in the quality of our leadership is our vision. If we do not have vision, we cannot lead.

As leaders with vision, we apply our ability to see potential, to see the future, to see beneath the superficial, to see progress.

When we connect with vision, it creates an empowering momentum inside us, fuelled by hope in the possibility that things can change.

As we begin to capture the dynamic of vision and let it infuse itself into our leadership, it does not mean we deny the current reality of a situation. But it does mean we are able to imagine a preferred reality of the future. Vision allows us to elevate our thinking above the immediate circumstances, situations and facts in the environment around us that are informing our mind. We can dream of outcomes and successes that are not stymied by current limitations as to how they will be achieved. Vision brings us fresh inspiration by outlining to us how the impossible can become possible and breathes life and hope into seemingly dire situations.

Vision is an essential leadership quality that allows us to see our desired destination from our current location and set a path and direction toward it.

The Power of Vision

All significant initiatives seen on the earth were created twice. Firstly, in the mind of a leader and, secondly, in the natural environment.

Academic and author Burt Nanus reported in his book *Visionary Leadership: Creating a Compelling Sense of Direction for Your Organization* that in successfully transforming organisations, vision is a very powerful tool for creating direction.

Nanus cites four main forces that leaders who cast vision release: attracting commitment and energising people, adding a meaning to their work, establishing a standard of excellence, and bridging the present and future.[11] Not thinking only in terms of the 'here and now', operating within the boundaries and paradigms of the current environment, when we function as leaders with vision, we access a future world we can move toward that supersedes today's status quo, pushing it aside.

IT entrepreneur Bill Gates had the foresight to envision the widespread use of his computer-operating system; flight pioneers the Wright Brothers saw a world with air travel; and architect Jørn

Chapter Three – Vision

Utzon saw the now-iconic Sydney Opera House in his mind when there was just a bare parcel of land on the Sydney Harbour. As reported on The Opera House website, his son said of his father:

> *He lives and breathes the Opera House,*
> *and as its creator, he just has to close his eyes to see it.*
> —Jan Utzon

The structure was created in Jørn Utzon's mind, and then that vision was made manifest into reality with construction materials.

Without a strong mental image operating in us that we can lock onto and use to pull us forward, we can become shut down, caged in by negative, limiting forces such as our feelings, our circumstances or the prevailing culture of our environment. Fear and unbelief can limit us, failure can intimidate us, a lack of immediate results can discourage us, and other people's negativity can stop us. But vision lifts us above those influences, attaches us to a new future and pulls us forward toward our dream and past our doubts and fears.

> *Make your vision so clear that your fears*
> *become irrelevant.*
> —Anonymous

Vision is demonstrated in the ability of parents to look at their children and see the strengths and talents of what they can become in the years ahead, not just the faults and limitations that may create frustration today.

Andy was a thirteen-year old who loved playing soccer with friends and family in the backyard, and he was very good. But in formal competition his initial attempts had been complete failures. He miss-kicked the ball, scored an own goal and got elbowed in the face by an opponent, leaving him benched, bloodied and devoid of any confidence or belief. Despite desperately wanting to play, Andy rejected future invitations to join other teams, believing he just wasn't good enough.

Andy's dad William though, looked past the obvious shortcomings of Andy's initial performance, and his statements that he 'wasn't interested' in playing. He knew that once Andy got over his confidence slump, he would flourish. William gave Andy some fitness and skills exercises to perform in the backyard, challenging him to continually improve in them, and Andy relished the competition to beat his own records.

One Saturday morning Andy and his dad drove to a park, where unbeknown to Andy, William had arranged for the high-school head soccer coach to run Andy through a personalised training, alone. The drills happened to be the same ones Andy's dad had set for him as Andy's dad had spoken to the coach months ago, asking for a training regime.

Andy excelled in the drills and earnt high praise from the coach. After several weeks of anxious hesitation, Andy rejoined the team. He went on to have a stellar career, representing his region and even playing internationally.

Andy's dad was able to look past the failure and see the potential that existed within his son. As leaders, when we exercise vision, we have the ability to identify and call forth the potential in others that may otherwise stay locked up and unrealised forever.

In November 1994 former Navy mechanic Gordon Bethune was appointed CEO of Continental Airlines. 'What they didn't tell me was that the engines had died and the tail was falling off', he joked.[12]

Continental had twice faced bankruptcy, was losing $55 million a month and ranked last in every airline-industry performance measure. The carpets on the planes were filthy, duct tape was used to hold overhead luggage bins together, and mechanics had to be flown from interstate to perform repairs, while the passengers sat and waited.

But Bethune had a vision that few of the ten previous CEOs over the last two years did. He immediately energised the company's culture by launching his bold 'Go Forward Plan' focused on 'flying to places people wanted to go' and bringing staff and management onto the same page.[13]

Between 1994 and 2004 Bethune's vision propelled Continental's stock from $2 to $50 a share, built a $650-million cash cushion, was consistently ranked in the top airlines for customer satisfaction and in 2004 was ranked by Fortune as the No 1 Most Admired Global Airline.[14]

When we activate the power of vision, it simultaneously lights a fire inside us that shuts down the voices of insecurity and doubt; by the same token, it brings fresh inspiration and hope to those connected to us.

Vision is something we can all do with more of, more often! As leaders, it's unlikely we will ever have too much!

Vision and Leadership

If we are without vision, we are stuck in the confines of the facts of the current situation, with no access to an energising preferred reality.

> *Leaders are limited by their vision*
> *rather than by their abilities.*
> —Roy T. Bennett

If we don't have a vision and a destination to move towards, it's difficult to make any strategic or progressive forward growth, or take anyone with us. Firstly, because we can't see where we're going. Secondly, we have not even comprehended the concept that there is anywhere else to go other than where we are today.

We are then reduced to the limitations of the reality of the current situation. We see only what those around us see.

Our role as leaders is not to keep people where they already are, but to take them somewhere new.

Vision, or seeing a better future than the present and seeing what others cannot, provides us with the raw material resources to inspire and lead others to this new destination. It is the substance we can draw on to communicate hope, describe opportunities for change and build expectancy about how life *could be*. This future picture also empowers us and others to push through the tough times, volunteer to make sacrifices and endure the hardships, knowing there is a brighter future ahead.

Our Personal Vision

When we don't have any forward vision operating in our own life, we tend to live in the familiarity of the status quo. We create an atmosphere that encourages those around us to conform to what we are comfortable with.

But as we connect with vision, allowing it to fill our mind and heart, we start to see differently. The change of frequency of our own internal dialogue is reflected in how we speak. It impacts those around us by encouraging them to move forward with us, even igniting their own vision percolating inside them.

The Evidence of Vision

One of the easiest ways we can measure whether we are leading with vision is to listen to what we are saying, because what we see in our mind will dominate our speech. How we speak about things is a reflection of how we view them.

If we have not captured a vision about our activity or the initiative we are involved in, our speech will reflect 'business as usual'. But when we capture an inspiring, passionate, optimistic vision, this energy will permeate our explanations about the situation and the opportunities.

If you can see it in your mind you are going to hold it in your hand.
—Bob Proctor

Communicating Vision

Communicating our vision allows us to function as a broadcasting station, emitting a frequency that others can pick up, tune into and begin to engage with.

People are drawn to us as leaders when we can communicate vision, as we can articulate how things can be (inspiration), not just how they are (information). This message creates hope and excitement.

When civil rights activist Martin Luther King Jr. famously thundered, 'I have a dream!' in his 1963 public address calling for an end to racism, what he was really saying was, 'I have a vision!'

And his vision was of a society that was so clear in his mind he could describe this reality in finite detail—what it looked like, how people behaved in it, how society functioned in it . . . and the more he verbally created this alternate reality for people to see, believe, enter, support and participate in, the faster the momentum built that started to bring that reality to pass.[15]

Transferring Vision

As leaders with vision, we can imagine and capture a picture in our mind, cast our vision through our communication, and effectively sow the image we carry into the hearts and minds of others, who—based on the same picture—can then run forward with us. This communication is the first step in *vision transfer*. When those who have captured our vision in their heart are then able to establish it in another person's heart again, this is the second stage of the process of vision transfer.

The Absence of Vision

The absence of a dynamic vision operating in our life typically results in the atmosphere around us and those connected to us becoming stale.

Without the overarching context of a compelling preferred reality to move towards, all we have is the *i*'s to dot, and the *t*'s to cross. We become consumed by a focus on *doing everything right* instead of *doing the right thing*.

> *Where there is no vision, there is no hope.*
> —George Washington Carver

Chapter Three – Vision

Born into slavery in Missouri in the mid-1860s, George Washington Carver was kidnapped, along with his mother and sister, when he was only a few weeks old. Moses Carver, the slave owner, succeeded in having the infant found and traded one of his best horses to get the baby returned. He then took over the responsibility of rearing George, including teaching him to read and write before he proceeded to formal education.

George displayed a brilliance in the field of agricultural science, a field he earnt a master's degree in 1894, the first African American to do so.

Carver was passionate about helping poor farmers grow their own food. He had an idea to use his expert knowledge of soil nutrients, gained from a young age on the Carver farm, to show others how specific crops could be grown for food while at the same time restoring the soil quality. This rotation system allowed cotton to be planted again a few years later. His vision to apply his unique skillset, his understanding of farming and his education stabilised the livelihoods of entire communities and generations to follow.[16]

In 1977, Carver was elected to the Hall of Fame for Great Americans.

Without vision, we can become legalistic, substituting the need to simply keep everything in order for passion-fuelled endeavour. Minor issues tend to receive disproportionate energy and attention, purely because there is nothing significant happening to invest our energy into.

When stuck in a maintenance pattern, we repeat habits and personal or corporate rituals. Even though time moves forward and the environment around us changes, at the risk of becoming irrelevant or ineffective in the current climate we stay mostly the same.

While the idea of keeping everything just the way it is can be a comforting thought, the reality is that most things in life are very dynamic. In nature, for example, everything is either growing or dying; nothing—whether the movement is visible to us or not—is stationary for long. Life is moving, and if we're focused on standing still, chances are we're actually going backwards.

A vision focused on keeping everything in its current state will produce a particular set of priorities, while a vision to proactively develop, shape, engineer and revolutionise our environment will manifest itself in a different lifestyle and type of behaviour.

The board of the regional newspaper *The Community Pulse* is tasked with setting the strategic direction and vision of the organisation, while the management runs the operation. The newspaper is funded largely by annual station memberships and donations and relies on volunteers to do all the little things such as social media posts, newsletter mail-outs and cleaning, to make it run.

However, as there are simply not enough bodies to do enough jobs, the line between the board setting the vision and the management implementing it gets blurred. Board members are then drawn into helping with hands-on tasks, such as stuffing envelopes for mail-outs or assisting in the catering for the annual general meeting.

The demand to help with operational tasks often makes it challenging for the board to stay focused on the vision and big picture of directing the paper. Board meetings often spend considerable time on important, but not strategic issues, such as the potential colours of the new logo, payment of bills or placement of safety signs in the office. This leaves little time or energy to focus on key board functions, such as 'What is the strategic direction of the paper?' 'How can we improve our impact on the community?' or 'What is the message and values of the paper?' The board, entwined with routine tasks, had lost connection with the higher, overarching vision; the 'why' of all the activity. As a result, the paper had developed a 'maintenance' type atmosphere.

Recent discussions with long-time employees highlighted the shift in focus. The members explained to the board that fifteen years ago at the paper's inception, they were inspired by the founders' vision of the potential of the paper: what it could achieve and how it would connect like-minded readers. The seed of that vision, still alive, was the reason they were involved today.

The board, reflecting on this feedback, quickly reconnected with the power of the pioneering vision, consequently breathing new life into the organisation; the result was, they attracted new advertisers and skilled volunteers, in addition to forming new partnerships in the community.

We need to constantly connect with our vision, be inspired by it to reinvigorate our thinking, raise our eyes above merely seeing the daily grind of maintenance tasks that can consume our time and energy, and elevate our thoughts to dream of what's possible—the end goal.

The Unfolding of Vision

It's not often that we develop an immediately complete, crystal-clear mental picture of a vision straight away.

Our vision is typically progressively clarified and adjusted, so we needn't be discouraged if we don't have a full 20/20 picture of it immediately. We might have a glimpse, a feeling or a concept of what we see or what can be in the future, but we need to work with what we have today.

> *If you can't see very far ahead, go ahead*
> *as far as you can see.*
> —Dawson Trotman

Sam had no awareness in or knowledge of politics through most of his young adult life. However, after he began to notice laws that were being passed and the legislation that went into effect, he developed an interest and took the initial step of joining a party he felt represented his values. After time he attended a meeting in his region. Continuing to develop an awareness and interest and regularly attending meetings, he was nominated for an officeholder's role at his regional chapter. Today, he has a leadership position at the state level and presents his views and those of constituents at national conventions, votes on party policy and discusses strategic direction amongst colleagues. 'I can now see where I need to take the party in the future, but when I started out, I just wanted to be involved in some way', he said.

Sam's journey into political leadership is a great illustration that our role as a leader can progress step by step; we can keep moving forward, one stage at a time.

As we take our first strides toward making our vision a reality, the clarity of where we are headed will increase. We can develop it, build it and allow it to grow on the inside of us. A big dream can still start in small beginnings; it doesn't require us to have all the details before we start moving towards it.

Vision's Impact on Our Use of Resources

The presence or absence of vision in our life will impact our approach to utilising the resources at our disposal. Consider the example of a pristine motor vehicle housed in a garage. If we are not connected to a strong vision operating in our life, we may well see that car only as an asset that needs to be preserved, maintained, well-polished and kept safe.

The resource, in effect, becomes its own purpose, and the vision for the car is to simply preserve it. We effectively see the resource as an end to itself.

However, with a sense of vision operating in our life, we're still concerned about looking after the car, but we also see it as a resource that can be used to achieve our goals. If the vehicle can't help us do that, we may instead just get rid of it and get one that can. Or trade it in for something practical that can help us achieve our vision.

We would think it more appropriate that the resource is used to achieve the vision, even if it meant arriving at the finish line with a few dings and scrapes rather than to miss reaching the goal but have an immaculate vehicle sitting idle doing nothing.

Resources such as money, possessions and buildings are seen in part as a means to an end to a leader with vision, not just an end in themselves.

Vision, Momentum and Direction

Have you ever tried to turn the steering wheel of a stationary car without the engine running?

Have you ever tried to push a stationary car?

There are two essential principles relating to vision we can take from these two scenarios:

i. **It's hard to steer something that's not moving.**

It's almost impossible to wrench the steering wheel of the vehicle with its full weight sitting squarely on top on the wheels while it is stationary with the engine turned off. When the car is moving, though, it's much easier to turn the steering wheel and direct the vehicle.

When we are functioning with a strong vision inside us and moving forward, it's easier for us to make changes in direction. If we're not moving at all, it's tough to change course. We can be essentially stuck, unable to move. It's almost impossible for us to follow a specific direction without momentum at work to enable us to turn the steering wheel.

The momentum we develop when we start to connect with vision creates an agility. It provides the ability to manoeuvre and change direction. It enables us to avoid obstacles, take advantage of opportunities and detour to connect to others who will support us, helping us to reach our destination.

ii. **It's harder to get something moving than to keep something moving.**

Initially, trying to push a stationary car is like pushing a dead weight. It feels like it's going nowhere, despite all our effort. However, once we get behind that car and start to exert energy, and just ever so slightly get the wheels turning, as the vehicle begins to move off its spot, the easier it becomes to get the tires rolling and car accelerating.

When we are stationary due to a lack of vision in our life, escaping the prison of habits and the status quo can be extremely challenging.

Getting started, just like moving that car initially, is the hardest part. However, when we begin to connect with a compelling vision and can take even the smallest of first steps forward, we begin to break free from the dead weight keeping us stuck in our rut.

*You don't have to be great to start,
but you have to start to be great.*
—Zig Ziglar

Once we begin, we generally find it easier to take the next step, and then subsequent steps after that as we build momentum that can carry us forward with less effort than when we started.

Aspects of Vision

What we see will determine what we believe. What we believe will determine our behaviour. And all of these together will influence the quality of our leadership.

There are several aspects of vision that are important to cultivate:

i. A vision of ourselves

What do we believe about ourselves? Who are we? Why are we here? What are we capable of, and what will our future look like? If we don't hold a healthy, dynamic internal vision of ourselves, our life and our potential, it will be difficult to develop a strong concept of the impact we can have. Empowering ourselves with thoughts of our preferred picture of who we are, who we are becoming and what we are called to during our lifetime is the starting point for us in the area of vision development.

> *As he thinks in his heart, so is he.*
> —Proverbs 23:7

ii. A vision for others

To grow as an effective leader, we must develop the ability to see the strengths and potential in others, the positives they can bring and the contribution they can make. If we primarily see the negatives and limitations of others or are continually frustrated by their present-day shortcomings, we can never be the sort of leader who equips and empowers others to rise to greater heights. It will also be difficult for us to inspire others to invest in our corporate vision.

When we accept that everyone (including ourselves!) has imperfections but can also see a preferred reality for them, their family and their future, we begin to create an environment for them to grow and develop in.

We may be the only one who sees their potential. They may not even see the potential that lies dormant inside themselves. Perhaps they are stuck behind the walls of a negative self-image, focused only on their weaknesses. As a leader, we can start to communicate what we envision for them and what we see in them, building a bridge that they can begin to step across, moving from their current place of restriction to a place of growth.

Leaders see, if they choose, the best in others. Without vision, as leaders we will only ever believe that 'more people means more problems', but with vision, we call forth the potential in others.

Chapter Three – Vision

iii. A vision for our community

What do we see about the values our community carries? What's *normal* in our community or society, but not necessarily healthy, that we may be able to change? What's missing that we could play a part in adding? How do we, in terms of leadership, provide for, protect and serve people in our community? How can we reshape the current culture and move towards a vision of a brighter future?

As we mature and grow as a visionary leader, our focus changes. From reaching our potential, we move towards helping the people and community around us reach their potential.

Dimensions of Vision

As mentioned at the start of this chapter, the concept of vision has several dimensions that in our leadership we need to understand and develop. Two critical aspects are below:

i. Insight—the ability to see into situations, to see under the surface and discern the reality of circumstances.

Leaders with insight can see the underlying, hidden patterns, issues and dynamics of a situation, not just the visible tip of the iceberg.

> *The best vision is insight.*
> —Malcolm S. Forbes

Online streaming giant Netflix has built their business on the ability to capture insights about what their customers watch, when they watch it and what their typical search patterns are.

The clarity this insight provides them results in 80 per cent of Netflix customers following their viewing recommendations, and a 93 per cent customer-retention rate.[17]

Insight allows us to build with great accuracy, address the key issues that are influencing a person or situation and address foundational needs.

Sometimes a circumstance may appear to be immovable – unchangeable, given the people, norms, history and trends of that particular environment. But when we have well-developed insight, we are able to discern the invisible behind the visible. This ability allows us to apply the correct key to unlock the situation, and the right strategy and remedy to each specific scenario, successfully navigating through the environment we are operating in.

ii. Foresight—the ability to see into the future

While most of us can recognise the situation as it currently is, leaders with vision also can exercise foresight. We can see things as they can be, or as they are going to be, tomorrow. It doesn't mean we need to get involved in tarot card readings or crystal balls. But it does mean that we can apply discernment as we watch the trends, review history, imagine the future, and we can put together the pieces of the jigsaw to give us a better sense of how the future is likely to unfold. This dynamic enables us to see the potential future of a person, relationship, situation or social environment and then plan for it.

Rhonda was a single parent, raising two daughters, eight and ten. She knew the rate of teenage drug use and abuse in her community was staggering, with devastating results. Rhonda began proactively arming her children with a defence strategy to overcome the inevitable peer pressure, educating them on the science of what drugs do to the human body, the pain of addiction and the destruction of lives. She connected her children with older teenagers, young adults and father figures who were strong, positive role models; they became reference points for her children, who adopted their values and standards. And she filled their weekly routine with fun, challenging activities, providing them a healthy environment to grow in.

Rhonda's foresight provided as much defence as possible to equip, protect and arm her children and reduce the threat before it reached them.

When engineers design a bridge, they assess the highest level of force the bridge will be required to withstand, taking into account the prevailing winds, the weight of traffic and span of distance—all factors that impact on the stress exerted on the bridge. They then design and build the bridge with sufficient strength to stand against those forces.

In the same way, when we see with foresight, we are able to anticipate the pressure that will come against our family, team, business or community—and not be caught off guard. We can begin to build the finances, relationships and processes to withstand those forces.

Vision is seeing a future state with the mind's eye.
Vision is applied imagination.
—Stephen Covey

Vision and our past

As we journey through life, the unfortunate reality is that we often encounter negative experiences such as defeat, loss, failure, hurt and unmet expectations. That's life. No one walks through unscathed. These incidents can occur as one-off events or over a sustained period; in one specific situation or across a broad range of circumstances.

It's important to acknowledge this reality, as if not handled accurately, these past adverse events can create long-term damage to our soul and mind, wounding us to the point that they become an impassable hurdle or inescapable pit. They can keep our life locked in the past, recycling previous failures or negativity, unable to move beyond them into the freedom and potential of our future.

If we cannot escape the pain or offense of these events, the trauma becomes hardwired into our emotions and psyche. It becomes impossible for us to break free, to look forward and cultivate a new dream and vision for tomorrow. It severely limits our capacity as leaders.

Organisational psychologist Dr Ben Hardy, whose blogs have been read by over 100 million people and featured in New York times and Harvard business review, wrote in Medium that, "In 2005, the National Science Foundation published an article showing that the average person has between 12,000 and 60,000 thoughts per day. Of those, 80% are negative and 95% are exactly the same repetitive thoughts as the day before.[18]

If we do not break this pattern of constant negative energy at work in our own life, it becomes a dominating negative influence, causing us to look back at what *didn't* work, thus shutting down any hope or vision of a better future. It's like trying to drive our car forward when we're always looking in the rear-view mirror.

Chapter Three – Vision

A man without a vision for his future
always returns to his past.
—P. K. Bernard

We also need to realise that daring to dream, with the courage to believe in a vision, can make us vulnerable to disappointment if things don't go to plan. It's therefore essential we handle the pain of possible setbacks effectively. Managing these negative instances well and moving past them involves some critical steps, such as those below:

- acknowledging the pain and disappointment
- finding the key learning from the experience
- affirming ourselves and finding a mentor to validate us and our value as a person
- accepting that failure is part of our journey toward success
- disciplining our disappointment, regrouping, and determining to move forward and try again.

These steps will help break the hold of the negative experience over us, assisting us in resolving the issue in our heart, allowing us the space in our soul and mind to start to dream and develop vision in our life again. They may also assist us in reviewing and, if necessary, adjusting our behaviour and the boundaries or the protocols we have in place to prevent repeating those experiences.

Vision and Strategy

When our vision is clear, with a level of detail, it enables us to build towards it strategically, one step at a time. If our vision is blurry or confusing, it's hard to know where to start or what we need to do.

John is a building project manager who constructs residential, commercial and industrial properties ranging from single-bedroom units, to multistorey office blocks. The common denominator to all his construction work, though, is that before he begins, he ensures he has a complete set of design plans to review and assess the intended project ahead of him. 'The plans provide a blueprint that details precisely how the structure will be physically built', he explains. 'The plans allow us to calculate quantities, materials, resources, plant, equipment and people needed to complete the final structure and how they will interact during the process'.

The same is true for us when planning to bring our vision to reality. The more precise the blueprint, the more it allows us to develop a strategy to bring it to pass. A lack of a clear vision and associated plan drastically reduces our chances of success.

Our strategy may range from a couple of to-do items over a week, to numerous projects spanning ten years. Regardless of the size or complexity, we need to give ourselves the best chance of success by spending some time designing and documenting a strategy.

Failing to plan is planning to fail.
—Alan Lakein

Raising some healthy questions we may not have contemplated, this process enables us to devise solutions to obstacles we hadn't considered.

We may not always choose to follow the plan to the letter—we may alter it as we go along—but the point is, we have a reference point (or points) that we, and others, can refer to on the journey.

If we can communicate the strategy to achieve our vision to those we are connected to, outlining some essential steps, it provides a greater sense of assurance and hope. People see there is a plan in place to reach the finish line. They know it is possible, even on paper. If all we can tell people is that we're just hoping it will work out, asking them to jump on board, it's harder for them to invest their trust, finances or hope in our leadership.

Activating the Power of Vision in Our Life

What's the VISION that you are locked onto for your life? What's your vision for yourself, your family, business, team or community?

Jonah's relationship with his dad was very fractured. While his dad clearly loved him, he displayed a range of negative behaviours that could have easily been offensive to Jonah, at times almost seemingly like a deliberate ploy to keep a wall up between them. But Jonah had a clear vision of the relationship he wanted; in his mind he could picture himself free of any negative response toward any of his father's behaviours or words. Rather, he imagined himself able to relate to his father, love him and move past any barriers and obstacles.

Jonah hung on to that vision for years, and slowly but surely built his capacity to live it out in reality by consistently initiating a strong, loving relationship with his dad. 'Thank you', his father told him one day. 'I was in a prison. I did not know how to escape from it or reach you, but you found a way through to me'.

As Jonah proved, we don't need a title to be a leader powered by the energy of vision. Develop a clear mental picture of your preferred future, think about it, write it down, stick it on your fridge, meditate on it and dream about it often. What will it look like to live in that place? What will it feel like, smell like? How will things be different for you, your family and the people around you? Write it all down so you can refer to it when you're feeling uninspired and have lost the energy in your journey (it happens to all of us at times).

Then be determined to stay on track!! Anchor yourself to your vision and practice living there in your preferred reality in your imagination each day. Start with a minute, then a few more minutes, then a half-hour, and keep building until you're living in that place even when you're going about your typical day. Allow it to pull you out of your current situation and into the picture of your future.

Allow your vision to start to spill over to affect your speech—don't say 'I'm overweight'—but instead, say, 'I'm losing weight'. Don't say, 'I can't', but rather, say, 'I can't ... yet, but I'm learning'. Tell every thought that opposes your vision it's a lie. Discipline yourself not to listen to it anymore. Substitute vision-focused thinking for it.

Learn to cast your vision out to others—start sowing it to individuals and groups. Start planting seeds in others who can catch onto your vision and possibly join you in support.

WARNING! Be careful whom you share your vision with when starting out. Don't disclose it to 'dream killers' who relish the opportunity to tell you, 'It's not going to happen' or 'You can't'. Choose someone who believes in you, has a compelling vision operating in their own life, and who will also be rational and truthful enough to give you some honest feedback.

Let your lifestyle reflect your vision—if your goal is to become a leader in a particular area, dedicate time, money and energy to train, practice and grow in that area.

The Power of Vision Leaders in Our Life

Sometimes it's the vision someone else has for us, or what that person sees in us regarding our potential and qualities, that can be our most significant source of direction and inspiration.

As a vision leader, we want to see the potential in others and speak positively about their potential to grow into the fullest version of themselves. However, we are best able to do this when we have experienced this dynamic in our own life, where we had a mentor who saw the type of person we could become. One who drew out our unique skills, characteristics and strengths that lay within us.

Often our leaders can find things in us that we don't see ourselves. Sometimes they may comment or highlight areas that at the time don't make any sense to us, or that we don't even agree with, but as time unfolds, their words can begin to line up and fall into place.

Connect with others who have a strong vision at work in their life, even if it's in a different area and focus from yours. It can help stir and draw out your vision.

CHAPTER FOUR

Prioritising Relationships

Relationship: The way in which two or more people or things are connected; or the state of being connected
Prioritise: Designate or treat something as being very or most important

R elationships are a crucial dimension of our life.

> *The quality of your life is determined by the quality of your relationships.*
> —Harvey Mackay

The area of relationships is also, unfortunately, often *misunderstood* and therefore commonly *mishandled* in our role as leaders.

The ability to prioritise the development and maintenance of genuine, meaningful relationships is a crucial ingredient to our leadership success.

When we do not prioritise relationships accurately, we will fail to be engaged or engage others in any significant way. If we do not develop meaningful engagement on a personal level through the conduit of relationship, making authentic heart connections in a family, workplace or community, it dramatically reduces our capacity to influence and lead others in that environment

If we underestimate the power of relationships within a family, team or organisation and do not foster these, we are less likely to have strong agreement amongst the individuals about our common values and standards, and less likely to have individuals contributing in a positive manner to the collective.

When we can facilitate, model and promote healthy relational standards we can build an unbreakable bond that will translate to a powerful impact on the environment around us.

> *The essence of leadership is relationship;*
> *influencing people to achieve things together*
> *that can't be achieved alone.*
> —Leonard Sweet

The Southern Renegades are a regional baseball team, playing in a semiprofessional league that is a feeder league to the national competition. The Renegades had for decades performed to a consistently high standard, achieving results that few teams rivalled, even those with bigger budgets and marquee name players. Team members often stayed with the club, despite taking pay cuts or a reduced role.

Opposing teams knew that when they faced off against the Renegades, they were going to be met by a ferocious, tight-knit group best known for their fighting spirit that set a standard for the league few teams could emulate.

Long-time team coach Ray explained, 'We build our team based on relationships, not performance. Being part of a regional community, we live and share our lives together outside of baseball, just as much as we do on the sports field. We're more like family

Chapter Four – Prioritising Relationships

than teammates, and our guys love being part of that environment. That's why everyone plays so hard, because they're playing for each other, not just themselves. That's the difference and that's why we're so successful'.

As leaders, when we can capture and cultivate the power of relationships amongst those we're connected with, the level of commitment and investment increases, and everything elevates to the next level.

Leaders of People

For fifteen years Monty was the senior financial officer in a private organisation. In effect, the second in charge of the firm to the CEO, he wielded a strong influence, with a large role in the decision-making. Not much happened unless Monty approved.

Monty felt that all employees, and his team in particular, were just 'positions on the org chart'—there to perform their job. He had no interest in developing staff and saw little point in any personal connection with them. As such, he would walk without acknowledgement past people in corridors, be dismissive as others were speaking, not respond to emails or calls from staff, and—without any explanation—simply not show up for meetings he indicated he would attend. He also used his position to interfere in projects without good reason, make ad-hoc changes to policy and procedure as it suited him, without even informing his team, and publicly highlighted employee errors as an example to others. Monty was great with numbers, but terrible with people.

Unsurprisingly, staff regarded Monty's behaviour as a 'power trip'. Transfer requests out of his team were not uncommon. As he held such a senior role, there was a considerable level of tension spread between staff and management. Based on history, staff were constantly wary of 'being ripped off' by Monty, not being paid for the amount of work they were doing, or being assigned an unachievable task when Monty was involved in the negotiations.

When senior management spoke of developing a culture of 'respect', it often drew raised eyebrows, as the staff saw no such behaviour being modelled from the top.

Despite any abilities Monty may have contributed to the organisation, his mentality and efforts regarding relationships meant he did a lot of damage to its culture, staff engagement and productivity.

How we relate to others as a leader, and as a person, always matters. We can be real pros at the technical aspects of our job, but our job always includes the people we interact with. When we as leaders do not treat others well, it detracts from a positive environment, affecting everybody.

We refer to some people as 'industry leaders' for their technical expertise or innovation. Some are labelled leaders because of the stature or influence they carry in a family, or a position or title they hold in the workplace. Others are hailed as leaders for being the most successful amongst their competitors. There are many ways to measure and determine a 'leader', but the type we are focusing on here can *connect with and lead people*.

When we are prioritising relationships as a critical component of our approach, we take the view that we are never actually leading an organisation, program, family, army or nation, because these are things. We understand that we don't lead things. We lead people.

Knowing this, we are never so naive as to assume that leadership can be reduced to the mechanical scheduling of human resources or overseeing the completion of tasks to a set deadline. Rather, we understand leadership involves human interaction.

> *Leaders understand the ultimate power of relationships.*
> —Tom Peters

If we're going to lead at home, in the community or in the workplace, we must be able to connect with others relationally so they can hear our heart, understand our thinking, express their uncertainty or request more information. This connection enables them to develop a deeper understanding of us, our vision and goals and allows us to appreciate their unique personality, situation, ambitions and concerns.

Douglas Ready is the founder and CEO of the International Consortium for Executive Development Research and senior lecturer at MIT's Sloan School of Management. His articles in the *Harvard Business Review* have set the agenda for leadership and strategic change over the last two decades. In his article titled 'Why Great Leaders Focus on Mastering Relationships', he argues that the ability to build trust through collaborative relationships is central to leadership effectiveness and is what distinguishes great leaders, from merely good ones.[19]

Relationships are the vehicle to share our heart and passion, to sow and grow our vision, to call out the potential within people, to touch and influence others with the fire and passion of our goals and message, and to extend our care and concern. As relationally focused leaders, we understand that in any pursuit, when all the activity, regulations, titles, programs, ceremonies, rules and contracts are stripped away, the only thing remaining will be relationship.

A boss has the title, a leader has the people.
—Simon Sinek

A good question to ask ourselves as leaders is, 'If I had nothing other than the strength of my relationships to rely on, would people stay with me?'

A Gallup poll of more than one million employed workers in the USA revealed that a bad boss or supervisor is the number-one reason people leave their job. In short, a large part of the time people don't leave their organisation, but to put more of a finer point on it, they leave their leader! Neglecting relationships or relating with people connected to us in an unhealthy or destructive manner has consequences.

Why relationships?

As leaders of people, we place a high priority on connecting, engaging, building and empowering the people connected to us, because we know that without the buy-in to our vision we cannot move the individual or the team forward. The idealised, stereotypical picture of the detached, aloof leader at the top of the organisational tree, executing corporate directives to the masses in solitude, never results in an empowered, engaged and loyal group.

Broken, dysfunctional or inappropriate relationships can become toxic influences and are a significant factor in the failure of many families, projects, and teams. Unfortunately, understanding the value and importance of relationships, and the art and commitment to developing them, is not always a focus amongst modern cultures. Research from 2017 showed the global divorce rate has increased by 252 per cent since 1960, alluding to the fact that in broad terms, the capacity of people to maintain relationships by resolving conflict and living for a cause higher than their personal fulfilment is declining.[20]

World trade disagreements, international conflict and global debt all present potential threats to our society. But the reality is that nothing threatens to undermine the health and functioning of individuals and our community more than the continual decline in our ability to establish and maintain excellent relationships.

The Role of Relationships in Our Life

Whether we describe ourselves as introverts, extroverts, socially outgoing or reclusive, studies continue to prove that people function better when involved in healthy relationships.

Tania-Marie was a bright, attractive, vibrant member of her inner-city community. She ran a successful business, owned a chic apartment, had a huge social network, attended celebrity functions almost every night and was frequently featured in the Social Times section of the city newspaper.

At night, after arriving home from the latest exclusive cocktail party or after-work drink, she would sit at home, alone, empty and sob. She didn't have a real friend in the world. She had reached the summit of her success mountain and attained status, material possessions and popularity, only to find there was nothing there but emptiness.

Without the soul connection to others to share her experiences with, Tania-Marie wondered if her life was even real at all. We know that human beings have a fundamental need for inclusion in group life and close relationships, even with a pet. Growing evidence in studies tells us that when our need for social relationships is not met, we fall apart mentally and even physically. There are adverse effects on the brain and the body.[21]

Assistant Professor Dr. Richard Martin's research into leadership and relationships in the work environment found that establishing strong relationships increases the effectiveness of the leader and thus the productivity of the organisation. Also, that meeting human needs is the premise of effective leadership—that to neglect the relational component is to neglect the higher-order needs of the members of the organisation. For both leaders and followers.[22]

When our leadership is shaped by understanding the significance of relationships to the lives of people connected to us, we have a definite edge in meeting needs. Also, in engaging others to join and support us.

The Impact of Relationship Breakdown

Given the importance of relationships to our well-being, the impact of relationship breakdown on our life is severe.

Due to the inability to relate effectively, businesses can fall apart, marriages end and governments grind to a halt. If relationships are not working well, it's unlikely anything else is.

The impact of relationship breakdown extends to many fronts . . . emotional, social and even financial. Findings in a 2015 UK study revealed that the national cost of family breakdown to the taxpayer is £47 billion, or £1,546 per taxpayer per year.[23]

Relationship breakdown and the lack of a close relationship are associated with an increase in adult ill health. Research examining a wide range of international data concluded that *'being in a quality relationship provides an emotional and social "protective effect" on an adult's health'*.[24]

Despite the *'me first'* culture being propagated in modern society, the sobering truth is that life was meant to be lived in connection with others.

> *It is not good that man should live alone.*
> —Genesis 2:18

When the increased frequency of relational breakdown is combined with its subsequent costs, it begins to paint a picture of society living in the shadows of this now-normalised giant.

As leaders who know the significance of relationships, we can begin to understand the relevance of connecting with people in a genuine and supportive manner. We can develop our ability to establish and maintain effective and constructive relationships with those connected to us.

The Other Side of The Relationship Coin

While the needs and benefits of developing healthy relationships are clear, the other side of the coin is that relationships, as explained above, involve people, and people, put simply, can be very challenging!

People can hurt us, let us down, expose us, intimidate us, betray us, undermine us, defy us and confront us. For many of us, the primary source of pain in our life has come through other people.

> *It's hard to trust when all you have from the past is evidence of why you shouldn't.*
> —Unknown

It is also likely that the people we connect with as a leader may well be suffering damage from previous negative experiences in relationships, or they place a lower priority on relationships than we do.

This combination of factors presents something of a paradox. While on the one hand, we understand the value of good relationships and desire them, on the other hand, we expose ourselves to two potential threats by pursuing them:

i. the pain (for example, from hurtful words, betrayal, judgment and criticism) that can be inflicted by people we enter into a relationship with
ii. the potential to become the recipient of the pain people are carrying from previous relationships

Vaughn was the coordinator of the local Men's Community Workshop, which provided tools, equipment and material for older men to apply their skills to create woodwork projects. Vaughan, a kind, gentle soul, always thought the best of everybody. Trying hard to create a social atmosphere in the group, he encouraged members to interact and make friendships, which was a key part of the program's objectives. To Gary he extended a generous, warm greeting when he attended his first weekday workshop. Gary responded well. However, at the end of the session, when Vaughan reminded the group to put their tools away, Gary took the remark personally and afterwards confronted Vaughan aggressively: 'I only left one screwdriver out!' exclaimed Gary. 'Why do you have to pick on me?'

Vaughan was bewildered by the attack, as he typically announced the same reminder at the end of a session. Gary continued to attend but was hostile to Vaughan, and tried to promote the idea, amongst other members, that Vaughan was not a good coordinator. Vaughan was so rattled he eventually resigned. Little did he know that Gary came from a broken home, with a trail of abusive relationships, and had left a path of accusation and conflict in every community group he attended over the last ten years. Vaughan was not the problem. Gary was. But Vaughn's inability to discern Gary's emotional baggage and create appropriate boundaries and accountability on Gary's behaviour ultimately cost Vaughan his job.

Engaging in relationships of any form can be a risky business. Engaging in relationships where we commit trust, energy and expectation to another person, and vice versa, can be downright terrifying—and fraught with danger.

Past hurts, negative experiences, unmet expectations and previous disloyalty can create internal wounds in us and a hesitancy to connect. It often results in our developing self-defence mechanisms designed to 'keep people out'. This response—to reduce the risk of further pain—is an understandable reaction, and in some cases, it is appropriate to draw certain boundaries around relationships with particular people. However, the same walls we put up to keep dangerous people out also separate us from good people with good intentions. These good people could well be potential partners we could build with.

While keeping people at a distance reduces the chance of being hurt and experiencing further wounds, it similarly reduces our ability to connect heart to heart. We can't share our dreams, shoulder each other's burdens, receive and provide honest and caring feedback, and receive inspiration from (or impart it to) anyone we are emotionally distant from.

It's hard for people to feel the flames of our passion, be impacted by the depth of our conviction or join the excitement of our vision if we keep a shield of protection permanently raised. They see us but can never touch us, and that is not a formula that creates strong followers or well-connected teams or families. If we take this approach, people may acknowledge us as occupying a leadership position or having a title. But without the reality of a personal connection, it will be difficult to genuinely influence them.

Previous Negative Relationships

It's extremely likely that at some stage, an issue in a relationship has arisen that has negatively affected or hurt us. It is also likely that we may have played a part in causing pain to someone else.

As leaders, we need to acknowledge this previous relationship pain, learn how to resolve it within ourselves and with the other party as best we can, and grow from it. We have to develop the capacity to cut off the ongoing impact of these negative relationship experiences in our own lives and continue to remain open to inviting and entering into relationship with others.

The beginning of your healing comes when you let out all the bitterness and pain, when you choose your peace over everything else and let them go.
—Unknown

Here are some useful steps to help this process along:

- recognising and acknowledging what has happened in the past

- not hiding from the pain it caused
- sharing the pain with a trusted friend
- seeking feedback on our behaviour and attitudes in the situation from a trusted and objective friend or mentor
- taking ownership for our part and apologising when relevant and appropriate
- seeking to restore the relationship where appropriate or possible, even taking small steps as a beginning
- resolving to forgive ourselves and others involved, and not letting it define us.

Without being unwise, we must learn to continually dismantle the walls inside our heart and walk free. Otherwise, safely behind the walls of our defence, we are isolated—limited in our ability to engage, connect and exert influence.

Developing a Healthy Relationship

No one is born an expert in relationships. It's likely in this area we need to undergo some training courses, seek the advice of mentors or ask for honest feedback about our relational style from those close to us.

All relationships are different, but if we want them healthy and positive, there are foundational building blocks that apply across the domains of business, family, personal or community life. When we understand these essential components, we can begin to build upon them strategically. In the same way that adding ingredients from a proven recipe will produce a meal of a certain standard, applying these components will significantly increase our chances of building a healthy relationship.

i. Caring

Caring is about us seeing and valuing the person first, then the role they perform or talents they possess second.

People don't care how much you know,
until they know how much you care.
—John Maxwell

As leaders, it's important we are committed to such things as achieving goals in the workplace or building our children's character at home. But we also need a high level of concern for the welfare of everyone in our sphere of influence. In short, we care about everybody connected with us. It doesn't mean we become emotional fretters consumed with making sure everyone is happy and comfortable. But it means we are supportive, invested and considerate of their personal circumstances. We are interested in providing opportunities to be recognised, grow, develop, and become successful in all aspects of their life. It means we care enough to have potentially difficult conversations about people's behaviour, mindsets or habits that may be limiting their well-being or effectiveness. Not to condemn or judge, but to support their growth and development.

In the workplace, for example, if we are overly focused on someone's performance or results but unable to see the person, or create an environment to grow in, it may mean we misjudge

Chapter Four – Prioritising Relationships

our role as leader. Only wanting results is taking a self-centered view, not valuing the employees appropriately. It would be no surprise if in this environment team members felt expendable, unappreciated, or if they provided a lukewarm response to our calls to contribute 100 per cent. If we view people as merely an appliance that performs a job, they are likely to act like one, fulfilling their role as directed but providing no additional heart effort to help us further.

ii. Accountability

The ability to take responsibility for our actions and to give a transparent report to others is an essential dynamic in creating a healthy relationship.

As we practice being accountable, we provide those connected to us a level of visibility that allows them to commit to higher levels of trust and confidence in us.

'Excuse me for a second', Matt interrupted his conversation with his work colleague Alan on their train ride home. 'What's up?' Alan asked. 'I just need to let Bronwyn know I didn't get to ring her mum today like I said I would'.

'Just ring her tomorrow. She won't know', Alan prompted.

'But *I'll* know', Alan smiled as he replied.

The higher the level of accountability between people, the greater the depth of relationship they can build.

Without clear accountability, either party potentially operates with an ulterior motive or in an environment of secrets. When people understand they are accountable to a certain standard of operating, a certain level of behaviour or a particular manner of conducting themselves, it also highlights that there are consequences if they don't meet these standards.

We don't always behave differently in public than we do privately, but knowing there is accountability in place certainly influences behaviour positively. Accountability can be the most significant preventative mechanism for misconduct creeping into practices, including our own.

When leaders fail to create accountability within individual relationships or groups, standards begin to drop, and the culture of the environment can deteriorate. Without any responsibility to be answerable for our actions, we, or others, can start to operate according to self-focused values and agendas, rather than those that put the family, team or community first.

iii. Grace

Grace is the ability to overlook imperfections and extend favour, not because a person earned it, but because we choose to offer it. It's when we treat people according to how much we value them, not how they have behaved.

We all make mistakes at one time or another. As leaders, we must understand that people never stop being people, and that means they are never perfect. It also means *we* are never perfect.

While it's reasonable to set expectations and standards in relationships around behaviours and commitment, loading people up with an expectation of perfection is a death trap to relationships and eventually burns the other party out. As leaders, we need to recognise that sometimes, despite a person's best efforts, or how badly we wanted something, people can drop the ball. Poor decisions are made, errors committed, and things go wrong. In these situations, punishing imperfection is punishing someone for being human, and it does little but push a sense of self-condemnation into the 'guilty party', driving that person further away. However, extending grace, support and understanding is an opportunity to strengthen our relationship and prove the level of commitment we have to them. It doesn't mean we don't address the issues at some stage and in some way, but sometimes our most significant opportunity as a leader to lift others is when they are down.

When we carry grace in our leadership, we have big hearts and an enormous capacity to love, forgive and help others through tough times, even if their actions have negatively impacted us. We can demonstrate excellent leadership to those connected to us by establishing this pattern.

We don't have to tolerate an 'anything goes' approach, but people around us need space to fail, to be imperfect and to know they are still accepted and valued, and that their relationship with us is still intact.

Elijah grew up in a middle-class home with parents who were extremely legalistic in their style of parenting. That is, their love and approval was dependent on his performance. If Elijah scored A's on his school report, he was celebrated and embraced by both parents. If he brought home a B, however, he received a starkly different response of stern words and cold distance until he redeemed himself with an excellent score next time.

As a young adult Elijah had it hardwired into his thinking that if he didn't perform, he was not entitled to love. As a result, unhealthily consumed with being 'good enough' to be accepted or approved of, Elijah was a perfectionist in all that he did.

But then Elijah started working with Ken, a friendly, middle aged, supportive fatherly type figure, in an architectural office. Ken was Elijah's boss but soon became a friend and significant mentor, both in and outside of work, whose friendship and input Ken valued tremendously.

On the day before a major presentation to a large client, Ken approached Elijah to query some of his work and they realised Elijah had made a significant error in his design calculations. Sitting at his desk, Elijah froze, paralysed with fear—tears welling in his eyes. In his mind, this would spell the end of their friendship, as he expected Ken to react with severe disciplining.

'Well, we better get that one fixed, mate', said Ken, who, glancing at Elijah, noticed his state of distress. 'Woah! What's up, sport?' Ken asked. 'It's just a blooper. We can fix it before tomorrow, and all will be well. Hey, wanna grab some lunch today?'

Elijah couldn't believe his ears and sat staring, shocked. 'But it's a big mistake—' he started. 'Hey', said Ken, 'you're a good architect. You just made an error. It happens. It happens to me all the time. But you've got to lose this idea that you've got to be perfect to impress me. I'll tell you a secret. I know you're not perfect, and you're not meant to be, and that's OK. All right? Now let's get this fixed and go get some lunch'.

It took Elijah months to process what had happened, but as the reality of Ken's grace toward him set in, Elijah began to break free of his fear that people wouldn't accept or value him if he wasn't perfect. Through this key event, and others that followed, he began to adjust his thinking and started to trust that his relationships were based on more than just performance.

iv. Truth

The fact is, if nothing's real, then nothing's real. If our relationship is based on pretense, falsity and pleasantries and all we're doing is trying to make each other feel nice, it's likely the relationship will lack any overarching strength of purpose or ability to stand up under pressure. If we're not honest about who we are, how we feel, what our opinion is or what our plans are, it's going to be difficult for anyone to connect with us in a meaningful way, because all they are interacting with is a shadow of our true self.

The level of truth in a relationship is, in some ways, an indicator of its strength. If we're in a relationship where we feel telling the truth would mean the end of the relationship, it highlights the maturity of that relationship is quite low.

However, when we can tell people exactly what we feel, not with the intent to hurt or damage, but purely in the interests of transparency and openness, and we know the relationship will stay intact even if the other person doesn't like what we say, it demonstrates a maturity, a strength to it.

Truth is not to be used as an attack weapon, nor is it to be hidden in fear of a reaction. Somewhere in that spectrum is a balance, dependent on the context. As the level of truth increases in a relationship where both parties trust each other to give and receive truth progressively, it further strengthens the connection and takes it to the next level.

v. Communication

In many ways, the only two tools a leader has are 'speaking' and 'listening'.[25]

Communication is the vehicle to inspire, align, learn, understand, clarify, direct, motivate, listen to and connect with. If we can't communicate with people, we can't build effective relationships with people.

> *The art of communication is the*
> *language of leaders.*
> —James Humes

As leaders, it's likely we overestimate our ability to communicate. Academic experiments tested the level of understanding subjects had when talking to people they knew well or, by contrast, barely at all. Researchers discovered that people who knew each other well understood each other no better than people who only recently met. To describe the widespread incorrect presumption that people we know well will understand us, psychologists created the term 'closeness communication bias'.[26]

> *The single biggest problem in communication*
> *is the illusion that it has taken place.*
> —George Bernard Shaw

'Just park in the other spot', Wendy advised her husband, convinced it was a clear instruction to move the car to the other side of the driveway, closer to the house, so it would be easier to bring the shopping in. When Wendy went out to the car, however, it was nowhere to be seen.

'I moved it to the other spot round the other side of the house', her husband explained. 'Isn't that what you meant?'

Chapter Four – Prioritising Relationships

To be an effective leader, we can never assume one-sided communication is sufficient for the other person.

Healthy communication patterns invite people to question and confirm, express their situation and feelings to each other, providing access to one another's perspective, struggles, fears and ambitions.

Communication provides the opportunity to make decisions based on the fact that all the information is available to each other.

i. The Power of Communication

Communication can be likened to the brushstrokes of a painting: the more brushstrokes, the more detail and the clearer the picture. When our communication is limited, it creates 'grey areas' in our relationships that can house and fester doubts, inaccurate interpretation and wrong perceptions.

Communication to a relationship is like oxygen to life.
Without it, it dies.
—Tony Gaskins

ii. Words Create Atmosphere

How we speak when communicating will create either a positive or a negative environment.

You can probably recall a time where you felt the mood of a room change for the worse when someone addressed a person harshly. Alternatively, you may remember where praise and encouragement created a positive, uplifting feeling. This happens because words have energy. They have the power to set an atmosphere.

Understanding the importance of *how* we communicate, as

well as *what* we say, is vital. When aware of this, we can tailor the tone, content, volume and speed of our speech, along with our body language, to communicate more effectively. A number of studies have been conducted relating to communication, and the general consensus amongst experts is that 70–93 per cent of all communication is nonverbal.[27]

iii. Listening and Hearing

You've probably heard the line about humans having twice as many ears as mouths, because we're meant to listen twice as much as we talk! Or more accurately, meant to 'hear'. We can listen, but if we do not hear well, we can take what is said out of context, or miss the heart, message and intent of the other person. This often-forgotten aspect of communication—hearing—is more important than speaking.

When Dominique asked his boss Paul if he could move desks, Paul told him to stop being demanding. 'Work from the desk you're assigned to', Paul said. What Paul didn't hear in Dominique's voice was the plea to move because workmates in his current location were bullying him.

Louise habitually stayed until closing time at the YMCA, long after her scheduled volunteer shift had finished. This aggravated the coordinator, Wendy, who suspected Louise was staying back to make sure she followed the closing procedures accurately. 'I just like to stay here as long as I can', explained Louise. What Wendy didn't hear was Louise's fear to return home because she was suffering an abusive relationship there.

'I'd love if we could allocate some budget each month to go on more dinner dates?' Abigail mentioned to her husband Zach.

'We've got to pay the gas bill before we go on posh dinners!' Zach reacted abruptly, with no suspicion that this was Abigail's way of asking for more intimacy. She would even have settled for an evening walk together after dinner just to talk.

If we're the type of leader who assumes we know what the other person is saying—we're just waiting for others to draw a breath so we can start speaking again—we may be limiting our ability to hear the heart of those connected to us, shutting down a valuable source of feedback that could help our relationship grow even closer.

Leaders who don't listen will eventually be surrounded by people who have nothing to say.
—Andy Stanley

We don't have to agree with or accept everything being said to us or give up the ability to make a final decision ourselves. Still, people need to feel they are valued enough that they have a chance to share their ideas, concerns and experiences with us at appropriate times along the journey. A consistently one-way dialogue is generally an unhealthy dynamic in any form of relationship.

iv. Overcoming the Translation Challenge

It's critical for us to grow in communication skills as leaders. This means continually asking ourselves, 'Am I speaking the other person's language?' Or 'Do they understand what I've said?' . . . 'Have I heard their heart in what they've communicated to me, or am I just assuming I understand them?'

Discerning Our Relationships

While we value all people, we also need to discern that some relationships have a different dynamic than others, as distinguished by their depth and purpose. And that's OK, as long as we can identify and acknowledge that.

Some relationships are just not meant to function in the same capacity as others, but that doesn't make the parties to them any less important.

If we're looking at someone as a partner to go all in with us and share our devotion to changing the world, but they are only interested in being casual friends, we're going to frustrate each other. Understanding this will allow us to realise the potential limitations or opportunities of each relationship and reduce the tension or risk of significant fallout.

When we develop this understanding, we can start to prioritise our time, adjust our expectation and the degree of trust we place in the different people we are relating with. It doesn't mean we need to exclude anyone from connecting with us; it just helps us put the relationship in perspective.

Relationship Killers

In the same way some key ingredients tend to make relationships work, several dynamics can have a severely negative impact on them. Here are some of the most significant relationship killers:

i. Offence

We choose to take offence. No one can just give it to us. The responsibility for taking offence is with us, the receiver, not the giver.

Chapter Four – Prioritising Relationships

Offence is one of the most common relationship killers and typically arises when our expectations are not met. It's something they said, did or didn't say or do that to us represents a personal insult or attack. It can have a range of impact on us, from being mildly irritating to making us feel like we've had a dagger put through our heart. But offence is a seed that, no matter how small it starts, grows on the inside of us and left unchecked will take root, develop branches, and bear fruit. Offence, when not dealt with, always results in the relationship growing apart. Offended people rarely settle with just parting company but will leave with the intent of bringing 'justice' to the situation and the other party.

> *The feeling of being offended is a warning indicator that is showing you where to look inside yourself for unresolved issues.*
> —Bryant H McGill

Some people are ticking time bombs in the offence stakes. With them, it's not a matter of 'if' but 'when' they will get offended. If it's not one thing, it will be another.

Peter was an intelligent man, married to wife Cathy and father of three children. He came from humble beginnings and worked hard in his corporate environment to progress his family's situation.

Underneath Peter's smooth, friendly exterior, he suffered from severe insecurity, being very sensitive in any dealings with others. It was not uncommon for him to feel deeply hurt by even very casual jokes, comments or behaviours that were not even directed at him or intended to cause offence. While he would laugh off the issue at the time, afterwards he would stew over it and determine to keep his distance from those people. He once avoided a long-time family friend for several years because he had picked a flower out of Peter's front garden and handed it to his wife as he was getting into his car. Peter felt this was disrespectful—that it was 'overstepping the boundary' of appropriate behavior.

This cycle was indicative of Peters pattern of quickly cutting himself off from those he felt slighted by, so they could not inflict any further pain. The people Peter took issue with were generally oblivious to the offence Peter had taken. Friends, family and work associates always felt a little unsure of Peter, knowing only that he could be warm and friendly one moment, then withdrawn, short, even angry the next, with no apparent reason for the mood change.

People tended to 'tread on eggshells' around him, careful not to accidentally touch any triggers.

Peter's pattern of easily becoming offended reduced his ability to maintain strong relationships, which reduced his capacity to lead or follow. Those who associated with Peter were respectful, but always a little on edge.

If we're leaders with a propensity to be 'offended', we are unlikely to engage and connect with others in a meaningful way.

The poison of offence can quickly seep throughout our entire being and undermine our relationships if we don't have the maturity and determination to manage it properly. When we mature in character, we reach a point where, instead of being offendable, we can quickly internally forgive and move on.

ii. Competition

A competitive spirit is not a bad thing. It may well be a contributing factor to our success as a leader. However, when we become driven by a compulsion—to compete with everyone, about everything—it limits us. It also potentially points to an unhealthy inner dynamic around our identity and sense of self-worth. If we are threatened or insecure by someone being better at something than us, we need to re-examine our motivation for competing and our fear of losing. If we are not internally configured accurately in this area, competition can end up driving our life and driving people away.

Never compare your journey with someone else's.
Your journey is your journey, not a competition.
—Unknown

Susan, the principal of a local high school of around nine hundred students and forty-five staff, had a reputation for always wanting the last word of any staff meeting, assembly or presentation, often duplicating what had already been said or adding unnecessary information to the point being discussed—always wanting to be the last voice heard so staff would recognise her as the leader.

Instead, her approach left them feeling oppressed and shut down whenever they spoke. Rather than using the staff's skillsets to the fullest potential and delegating some of the communication roles, she was determined to assume every role as the 'key voice' of the school community.

Susan's competitive approach ultimately silenced all those around her, as teachers gave up trying to communicate their message, knowing Susan would come in over the top of them anyway.

If we have an unhealthy disposition towards competition, we can end up suffocating those around us, driving away those who could help us the most.

Sometimes we just need to give people we're in a relationship with space to be who they are and what they do well. Why fight it? Sometimes others are good at what we are not. Allow them to be great at what they are great at. If we're both good at the same thing, we're not adding anything to the partnership anyway.

Being free to congratulate others when they do well and achieve success is a healthy place for a leader. If we can't congratulate others, we are essentially still competing with them, and constant competition creates limitations in relationships.

When competition overtakes us, our view of 'winning' can become distorted—and center more on beating the person next to us and less on the achievement of our life purpose and vision—and the two things are very different.

People achieve more as a result of working with others than against them.
—Alan Fromme

---

iv. Judgement

When we make a judgment against someone, we apply a legalistic measure and issue an internal verdict of whether they have passed or failed, or are right or wrong.

As the office coordinator of a left-wing political party, Theresa was able to quickly assess whether friends, family and community members agreed with her views. Theresa felt she had the right, and was even part of her role, to dictate or judge the views, values and decisions of others she knew. If people didn't agree with her, she would bombard them with her opinion of what they 'should support' and what they 'should believe' which obviously created resentment; people felt controlled and suffocated by her.

As leaders, we are violating the principle of relationship if we try to overpower anyone's human will. This approach does not produce positive long-term results.

There is no problem in objectively assessing someone's behaviour or views to determine if we agree. But if we make a judgement toward others that then shuts us off from relating with them, it will invariably limit our leadership effectiveness.

When you judge others, you do not define them,
you define yourself.
—Earl Nightingale

While we may not agree with people's views, behaviours or lifestyles, if we are mature leaders, we can still relate in a healthy and productive manner that keeps some form of relationship open with all people.

A Balance of Relationships

If the energy in our relationships is always about 'us', and 'our' development, and 'our' achievement, . . . it may indicate a distorted focus. We need a balance in our relationships of receiving and giving, across all aspects of work, family and community life, which involves three levels:[28]

i. Those ahead of us—mentors
   People we are accountable to and can draw from, who take us higher in life

ii. Those at our side—friends
    People we can confide in, be real with and enjoy companionship with on the journey

iii. Those behind us—protégés
     People we can support, empower and guide to help them grow

CHAPTER FIVE

Persistence

Persistence: The act of continuing in an opinion or course of action in spite of difficulty or opposition

True leaders never quit.
Persistence is the ability to stay continually committed to a task or a cause, despite opposition, a hostile environment, difficult circumstances or personal criticism, over an extended period.

We can do anything we want as long as we stick to it long enough.
—Helen Keller

We can be talented, present well and have good intentions, but if we don't have the inner quality of persistence, we can soon get knocked out of the leadership race. We ensure our own defeat when we give up and stop.

Persistence is an internal choice. It's not an opportunity afforded us by someone else.

In her *New York Times* bestselling book, *Grit: The Power of Passion and Perseverance*, Professor Angela Duckworth outlines her premise that 'what really drives success is not 'genius' but a special blend of passion and long-term perseverance'. [29]

As a professor at the University of Pennsylvania, Duckworth created her own 'character lab' and set out to test her theory.[30]

From surveying soldiers completing boot camp to assessing teachers in rough neighbourhoods, to interviewing sports coaches and CEOs, she concludes: 'It's all about what goes through your head when you fall down', she says, 'and how that, not talent or luck, makes all the difference'.[31]

Once we develop persistence, we have an *internal dynamic* that *refuses* to stop. A passion and a determination in us will never give up and never give way to what's opposing us . . . even if we seem to be losing the fight or not making progress. That powerful force called *persistence* enables us to overcome and triumph, to push through and reach our destination, even in the face of seemingly insurmountable odds.

Nothing in this world can take the place of persistence.
—Calvin Coolidge

Persistence is not a skill learned from a lecturer or an ability we acquire from reading a textbook. Persistence is the outward manifestation of a heart attitude. It's the evidence and demonstration of a deep conviction embedded in our inner being.

It's when we endure whatever comes up against us . . . whether it's betrayal, threats, sickness, fear or loss . . . we set ourselves on our target; we keep getting up when we get knocked down—and keep driving toward our dream.

There is no more powerful force on earth than when we take a 'do-or-die' stand in our own heart that no matter what the cost, the opposition or the pain, we're going to stick to the task we set our mind on, even to the point of exiting the planet permanently.

The Necessity of Persistence

The question we all face, when assuming any sort of leadership role in the home, community or workplace, is not *'Will adversity come?'* but rather, *'How will I respond when it does arrive?'* We need to accept the reality that no matter WHAT we set out to achieve in leadership, something is going to emerge that will potentially stop us if we let it.

Henry Ford had a pioneering dream to revolutionise the automobile industry yet went bankrupt twice before successfully designing his first car. Ford understood the value of persistence, however, and noted that *'When everything seems to be going against you, remember that the airplane takes off against the wind, not with it'*.[32]

He launched the Model T in October 1908 and over the next nineteen years sold fifteen million of these cars.[33]

It's hard to find an example of anything of note that came to fruition without enduring tests and overcoming adverse circumstances. If we quit, we forfeit our chance to experience victory.

To carry us in our leadership walk, we cannot rely on our title, our qualifications, our position or our well-meaning intentions, but rather something hardened and forged inside us that puts strength in our backbone and toughness in our gut, reinforcing our resolve.

Walt Disney was an eighth-grade dropout who faced numerous rejections as an artist. Newspaper editors told him he had no talent. He was even fired once for lacking imagination and original ideas.

In his father's garage with the help of a borrowed library book and loaned camera, Disney experimented with animation and launched his first animation company, which went broke within two years. Returning to work as an employee, he then had his first commercially successful character stolen by his producer, was rejected by bankers over three hundred times to fund production of *Mickey Mouse*, had his best animator stolen by his employer and then suffered a nervous breakdown. After regrouping, he started producing *Snow White and the Seven Dwarfs* in 1934, enduring four years of industry mockery that predicted an epic fail and publicly labelled the project 'Disney's Folly', during which time the studio went bankrupt. Finally completed and released in December 1937, it grossed $8 million (approximately $134 million today) and is still the most successful sound film to date. Disney's subsequent films earned him five Academy Awards. He established The Walt Disney Company, or Disney, a multinational media and entertainment that grossed over $65 million US in 2020.

When asked about the keys to his persistence, Disney remarked, 'All the adversity I've had in my life, all my troubles and obstacles, have strengthened me. Around here . . . we don't look backwards for very long. We keep moving forward'.[34]

Not content to be in the captain's seat of leadership only while it was all smooth sailing, in contrast when the wind blew, the waves got choppy, the boat started to pitch and the journey became distinctly uncomfortable, he exerted his determination the most.

In 2014 the Korean ferry *Sewol* sunk, killing more than three hundred people. Captain Lee Joon-seok, however, instead of issuing safety directions and emergency-response instructions, fatally abandoned ship while hundreds remained trapped inside.

Massachusetts Maritime Academy instructor and retired US Merchant Marines captain William Doherty explained that in these pressure situations, 'When the leadership cuts and runs, it leaves a vacuum that is almost impossible to fill'.[35]

As leaders with persistence, though, we commit to staying the journey. Sometimes the greatest need for leadership is when the storm is at its strongest and the outlook at its bleakest.

These are opportunities to provide exceptional leadership by standing right there during the battle—refusing to budge.

At the end, someone or something always gives up.
It is either you give up and quit, or the obstacle
or failure gives up and makes way for your success
to come through.
—Idowu Koyenikan

Being persistent does not mean we can never change our approach, never offer an apology, never seek feedback or be open to correction. While we can stand firm against opposing messages and circumstances that test us, we should always maintain a soft heart towards people. We can be simultaneously steadfast in our nonnegotiable stance on our beliefs and our determination to reach our goals, while still open to relationship and interactions.

We can see opposition as a normal process of the journey. And keep moving forward, even if we are pushed off track or delayed temporarily. We are always capable of exercising our choice to decide that this obstacle or setback will not stop us.

As an English teacher herself, Natasha was excited that in his schooling her young son Max would pick up her love of reading.

But right away, Max struggled. From the outset in the first grade, he found basic reading and writing challenging. Despite Natasha's tortuous attempts at supplementary home-teaching exercises using her traditional methods, Max progressed haltingly and often declared 'I am the dumbest kid in school'.

Natasha had a nagging feeling that something wasn't right. Pursuing a resolution, she poured through internet articles and websites late into the night, not prepared to accept that her son would simply 'miss out' on the joy of education. She had the school test Max for learning disorders, but they reassured her his results were 'about expected for Max' and to take solace he was 'a great kid, and she had nothing to worry about'. She refused to accept the verdict. When Max was in sixth grade, she took him to a specialist, where he was diagnosed with dyslexia.

Shocked, but buoyed, Natasha poured herself into researching the condition, quickly realising the traditional teaching methods were ineffective in this case. Through her investigations she found proof that effective methods existed to take children with dyslexia to high levels in reading. Then to help him at home, she arranged specialised tuition and retrained herself in dyslexia-appropriate teaching methods.

Max responded immediately. His confidence increased and he began to understand how the condition affected his learning, and how to get around it. Max graduated from university and is now a successful lawyer, a reading-dependant industry, in a prestigious law firm.

Sometimes persistence achieves what nothing else can.

We all have bad days, times of self-doubt and seasons of flatness, but when we carry persistence, we keep finding a pathway through.

We carry a heartfelt belief that the need to continue is greater than the costs, and that the benefits of achieving our goal outweigh the negative hurdles and potholes along the way.

This mindset empowers us like a buoy in the ocean, where no matter how big the waves that crash against it or how far it gets pushed down, the air in the buoy keeps causing it to rise to the surface and overcome the forces trying to sink it.

Persistence and Feelings

Persistence is not about continuing only when we are feeling good and 'up'. It's about, no matter what our emotional state, predetermining to stick to our beliefs and pursue our dreams.

I am not moved by what I see.
I am not moved by what I feel.
I am moved by what I believe.
—Smith Wigglesworth

If we live in a pattern where our fluctuating feelings are our primary source of truth, our degree of persistence can vary from day to day. For example, if we feel uncomfortable when something gets difficult, or we become despondent because something doesn't go to plan and we only refer to our feelings in *this* situation, then we're more likely to skid to a halt in the pursuit of our goal. But if we're able to move past our emotions, functioning on a higher level according to our deep, core beliefs and convictions, we are not focused purely on what we feel. We are now also focused on what we are pursuing, and we will likely demonstrate greater persistence.

Persistence Wins Out

Winning does not necessarily translate to mean we've been persistent. But showing persistence *does* mean we're winning.

Being a leader, we don't necessarily maintain a perfect win-loss record, sailing effortlessly to continual victory; we don't automatically remain unscathed by situations and we might have fears about the outcome of events in the future. But we have our eyes on the goal and, despite the hits and losses we take along the way, are determined that nothing will stop us from reaching it.

Courage is not the absence of fear,
but rather the judgement that something else
is more important than fear.
—Ambrose Redmoon

Sometimes, we lose. Sometimes we make mistakes. Sometimes we back the wrong horse. Sometimes we take a beating. These are not necessarily indicators of the quality of our leadership or a sound guide as to whether we should continue on in our journey. Leadership is about consistently showing up to take our place, even when things haven't gone to plan or we're experiencing pain. Being a persistent leader is about developing the ability to stay the course despite obstacles, fears, setbacks and failures.

It's not whether you get knocked down,
it's whether you get back up.
—Vince Lombardi

Researchers from the University of Pennsylvania showed that when their parents expended effort at a task and talked about the necessity of pushing through, even when things get hard, four and five-year-olds were more persistent than children who didn't see this behaviour modelled and encouraged.[36]

Sticking to a task, overcoming external obstacles, breaking through internal fears or enduring pain to cross the finish line is modelling a pattern of perseverance that those connected to us can draw on, applying it in their own life.

Persistence Overshadows Talent

The point where our skills and abilities finish is the point where our persistence takes over.

Persistence can overcome a lack of talent, unfavourable circumstances, or the odds that are stacked against us. Sometimes we aren't the most gifted, likely or favoured, but we don't need any of those things to be the most determined. Success and breakthrough often follow when we are simply more diligent, not more talented, than the next person. Our persistence can create a path when there is no way forward and push open doors that remain closed if we only give a half-hearted effort.

Regina and Nicole—both talented junior tennis players—always ranked number one or two in the state. Clearly superior to the other players in their age group, on any given day they were only competing against each other. Gashelle ranked below the two standouts. In her first few tournaments, both girls comprehensively beat her, but in response, she steeled herself to a dedicated program of coaching and training and committed to her fitness, her diet and her mental-preparation regimes. Whether it was cold winter mornings, hot summer days, weekends or holidays, she refused to miss a training, with her eyes set on the target.

Gashelle began to rise to the top of the second tier, her hours of uncompromising, determined training starting to show. Despite losing to Regina and Nicole, she kept training.

A year later Gashelle had her breakout tournament, defeating both Regina and Nicole, proving too much for the talented pair.

Many remarked how quickly Gashelle had improved, but she, her coaches and support team knew it had been a long, hard, persistent journey.

In the sporting arena, like this story of Gashelle shows, the most talented athlete is not always the winner. Sometimes the sheer refusal to surrender carries the day. There are many instances of sportspeople and teams who—through sheer determination and persistence—triumphed over more talented opposition.

In one of the most dramatic upsets in US history, the 1980 men's US Olympic hockey team, consisting of only amateur and college players, faced off against the might of the four-time defending gold medal winning Soviet Union, who boasted hardened professionals and some of the best hockey talent in the world. The US was ranked 1000–1 odds but took out an incredible 4–3 win. The game became known as the Miracle on Ice. Architect of the success, coach Herb Paul Brooks Jr., in a now-famous quote, explained the team's need for determination and persistence when he told them: 'You think you can win on talent alone? Gentlemen, you don't have enough talent to win on talent alone'.[37]

Soccer club Leicester City faced relegation from the English Premier League in 2015 and yet with mostly the same team overcame 5000–1 odds to take the title in 2016. Being driven by an insatiable hunger to succeed, they stunned the sporting world to become Premier League champions.[38]

Muhammad Ali was ranked a 4–1 underdog and considered too old at thirty-two when he claimed the boxing world heavyweight title in 1974 against Awesome George Foreman. Despite connecting with his ferocious punches, Foreman could not match Ali's sheer determination, which shocked Foreman as much as Ali's hits. Foreman recounted, 'I hit him hard to the jaw and he held me and whispered in my ear: "That all you got, George?" I realized that this ain't what I thought it was'.[39]

Nothing is more common than unsuccessful men with talent. Persistence and determination alone are omnipotent.
—Calvin Coolidge

A solid brick wall is not often broken down by one enormous and perfect hit from a sledgehammer, but rather by consistent, committed and repetitive blows. Persistence is often more potent than size and strength.

Building Persistence

Our level of persistence can vary significantly according to a range of factors. Research using the Temperament and Character Inventory and five factor model of personality suggests it can relate to our genetic makeup, a combination of our personality characteristics and our environment around us, or simply our learned behaviour.[40]

Some people have a natural resilience and ability to overcome a range of significant negative circumstances and setbacks. In contrast, for some of us, the smallest difficulty can result in instantly giving up.⁴¹

Vanessa Bennet, CEO and founder of Next Evolution Performance, who specialise in facilitating individual and organisational high performance, notes, 'Some people seem to inherently have the ability to be more persistent than others'. She qualified, however, that it 'is also something that can be a learned behaviour. So the good news is that you can develop it'.⁴²

For most of us, persistence is a characteristic developed over time and built through practical experience. Developing persistence can be a progressive process, formed within us as subsequent obstacles and limitations are faced and overcome. The ability to move past our immediate opposing force can establish a dynamic and foundation in us that enables us to face and overcome the next.

When we first encounter opposition and negativity, particularly in the public realm, it can be such a shock that it can scar us emotionally and mentally, just like any other traumatic event, and cause us to shut down and withdraw from the contest.

Unfortunately, sometimes the only way we really learn how to persevere is to be knocked over and left to decide whether we are going to get up and keep going. However, every time we rise, we increase our level of persistence.

If approached with the correct mindset, the same resistance that is holding us back can also be the catalyst to make us stronger as we learn to break through that situation. This momentum can propel us forward toward our destination.

A weightlifter will tell us that resistance is necessary to get stronger, and we know we have the wonder of flight without gravity.

Sometimes the only difference between the rock in our path being a blockage or a stepping-stone is the level of persistence we apply.

Nothing can replace the battle-hardened toughness we develop by being on the frontlines, persisting in the face of our internal struggles and external adversity.

Abraham Lincoln, one of the most heralded presidents of the United States, demonstrated incredible persistence before he was elected the sixteenth president. For thirty years in the lead-up to his election victory, he faced obstacles: he lost his job, his fiancée died, he failed in business twice, suffered depression throughout his entire adult life, had a nervous breakdown and was defeated in eight elections. However, he persisted despite all this and became one of the most revered leaders of world history. His tenure was highlighted as the first president to outlaw slavery forever. How would the world, and many people's lives, have been affected had he given up?[43]

Persistence and Failure

Failure will always occur, but failure isn't final. Mistakes and defeat are part of our leadership journey. It's not a sign that we should quit.

Anyone who has never made a mistake has never tried anything new.
—Albert Einstein

Failure can be a necessary part of our growth as leaders.

Persistence is never more required than after we have experienced failure.

Sporting champions often speak of the pain of a loss as strengthening their desire to come back and win the next one. Their failure at one point in time increased their persistence to achieve success in the future.

Failures, repeated failures, are finger posts
on the road to achievement.
One fails forward toward success.
—C. S. Lewis

Failure is a valuable feedback mechanism that can be used to sharpen our approach and cause us to rise to a higher level.

Thomas Edison failed 10,000 times before triumphing in the creation of the light globe.[44]

The first requisite for success is the ability
to apply your physical and mental energies
to one problem incessantly without growing weary.
—Thomas Edison

After each successive failure, Edison tried a slightly different approach. His failure informed his learning, with each failure allowing him to step closer to success. While his persistence remained steadfast, he was wise enough not to blindly repeat the same method that led to his previous failure. Our natural inclination to stop after we fail, and our inability to make adjustments after failing, can limit our ability to keep progressing toward our goal.[45]

The pilots of a plane make hundreds of subtle corrections

throughout the course of a journey based on the feedback they receive informing them they have 'failed' by veering ever so slightly off course. They do not respond to the feedback by changing their landing destination or abandoning the aircraft by parachute. They simply utilise the input to make slight adjustments to correct the plane's path to its original intended destination.

When a high level of persistence is operating in our leadership, we can receive feedback from failure and apply the learning, coming back wiser—even more determined and better equipped to reach our goal.

Most of us would probably admit that when we look back in hindsight at our leadership journey, we would have done some things differently. Some of those lessons are learned only through experience, but we can apply them only if we are persistent enough not to abort our leadership journey.

Sometimes as leaders, we can be at the cusp of a breakthrough, only to forego the victory because we decide to quit at the final stage. If only we knew how close we were to walking through to the other side.

The Message Persistence Sends

When we demonstrate persistence, we send a powerful message to everyone and everything around us that we are not easily intimidated and that we won't be opting out anytime soon. To those connected to us, this message provides reassurance, creating trust that we are committed to the task.

People will be watching us to see how much we believe in the message we're promoting. If they aren't convinced we'll stick around when the heat comes, their allegiance to our leadership will almost surely be lower than when they're confident we'll stay the course, no matter what. Why would people commit to go to war with us if they think we're likely to go AWOL during the battle?

For eight months during the World War II Siege of Tobruk, all that stood between rampaging enemy forces and the strategic Suez Canal was the determined 'Tobruk garrison' of the Allies, consisting mostly of Australian soldiers.

Surrounded by enemy forces, the Tobruk garrison withstood constant tank attacks, artillery barrages and bombings daily. They endured the extreme heat of the desert by day, the severe cold at night, the frequent frenzied dust storms, all the while living in dugouts and caves.

Despite these hardships, the committed defenders of Tobruk would not surrender, and they would not retreat, holding off the enemy against all the odds. Their doggedness and resilience achieved lasting fame when they were infamously labelled the 'Rats of Tobruk'.[46]

The Tobruk garrison continually shocked their enemy with the level of persistence they demonstrated, highlighted by the writings of a captured German officer, who stated, '*I cannot understand you Australians. In Poland, France and Belgium once the tanks got through, the soldiers took it for granted they were beaten. But you are like demons. The tanks break through and your infantry keeps fighting*'.[47]

Even the renowned German army strategist Erwin Rommel declared after witnessing their dogged tenacity, '*If I had to take hell, I would use the Australians to take it*'.[48]

Persistence sends a powerful message, including to our opposition.

Persistence Lays a Foundation to Build On

When we as a leader establish a standard of persistence, we become like a foundation stone. When another person later adopts the same footing and determines to stand just as we have, we've built something of strength and significance. As others join us, we grow into a formidable force.

If we simply leave the fight, someone has to come back to the same site we once occupied and start from the very beginning by re-laying the foundation stone of the campaign we waged or the message we declared. We may not feel at times that we are successful or that we are achieving much, but the key is that we are still occupying that space, and we are still a presence, providing a base for others to stand on, join us and take our work further.

Issues Affecting our Persistence

Even though we may understand that persistence is a crucial characteristic of our leadership success, our persistence may still be limited or undeveloped. Below is a range of factors that represent these potential stumbling blocks:

i. Our sense of conviction

Our degree of persistence can be an indicator of our real measure of conviction about an issue. If it's convenient or popular to show concern about a value, topic or situation, we'll probably be inclined to stick with it.

But if our stance becomes uncomfortable to maintain or unpopular, unless we really believe in it we're likely to drop it. Why hang on to something we don't care about if it's causing us pain? However, with true love, a deep conviction and a genuine passion in our heart, we'll hold it and keep pursuing it, no matter what the cost.

Daniel shared a post on social media disapproving of his local government's recent controversial decision to allow retailers to open on a traditional religious holiday. Having grown up in a religious family, he had tried to maintain a faith awareness for his children. Decisions like this, he felt, worked against an important part of family and community life, which should be a higher priority than just making a few more dollars.

However, not everyone shared that view. Daniel received harsh criticism from local community members and from business owners who felt he was 'shutting down the viability of their economy by wanting shops to stay closed'.

Surprised and a bit shaken, Daniel removed the post, not mentioning it again. He decided it was better to just stay quiet about these matters next time.

If we don't have a strong conviction about an issue, we can be quickly stopped in our tracks when we face opposition to our views.

ii. The weight of the majority

The majority may be represented through the media, groups, networks or general community opinion. Over time the sheer weight of the majority can wear us down and cause us to question whether it wouldn't be easier to just 'go with the flow'. These situations are where our persistence is tested.

As leaders we need to develop a level of comfort with the idea that we could be in the minority with our views and opinions. This doesn't make us wrong. Remember, everyone believed the earth was flat until the ancient Greeks started studying the stars and applying some science using sun dials.

> *It does not take a majority to prevail,*
> *but rather an irate, tireless minority,*
> *keen on setting brushfires of freedom*
> *in the minds of men.*
> —Samuel Adams

If we just went with the flow of the majority, we wouldn't be a leader, we'd be a follower. We need to understand that any tension we are creating in the environment because of our view is not actually a bad thing, as it shows we are having an impact and building an atmosphere for change.

iii. Focusing on the circumstances

The more we look at the barriers to achieving our goals, the more they grow and the bigger they become.

> *How you see the world depends on how you look.*
> —Kenneth Cole

If our reference point to decide if we should continue moves from an internal conviction, to an external analysis of all the rational, logical reasons why we can't succeed, our level of persistence will diminish.

Hellicy Ngambi grew up with the hope and excitement of attending the nearest school to her African village. But this meant, at the age of seven, crossing a fast-flowing river to the boarding school each week, carrying seven days' supply of food and clothing. Several of her friends were swept away to their death. She had to collect her own firewood to cook her own meals, fetching her own water to cook and wash in. To study at night, she had to make her own paraffin lamp from cloth. Today, a full professor of business leadership, she is the first female vice chancellor at a public university in Zambia.

'I thank God I persevered', Hellicy said. 'Now I can inspire other girls and women to not give up irrespective of the obstacles they face in life'.[49]

Our commitment to our goals, assignment and values shouldn't be determined by the outer circumstances, Instead, if we think it's right, then we should keep at it, even if it means facing overwhelming odds. If the underdog just never showed up, imagine the number of sporting events, elections and exams around the world that would simply be cancelled every day. As leaders, we need to be prepared for the fact that our circumstances are rarely perfect, but that can't become our determining measure of whether to persist or not.

iv. Loss of vision

If an overarching vision is motivating our activities—for example, conducting public meetings to gain support for social change, completing study to position us to move into a field we are passionate about, or instilling certain disciplines in the home to establish values in our children that will serve them well in life—the energy to persist can be eroded over time if we lose sight of that vision. When we get disconnected from that vision, we lose touch with the very power source that provides us with our renewed daily inspiration to keep going.

Losing vision is like driving our car to a particular place, relying solely on the GPS for directions. If the GPS loses the end-destination coordinates, eventually we just pull over and stop because we can't see where we're going.

In the same way, our level of persistence can be negatively impacted when we lose focus on the big picture, and we get caught in the 'grind' of the day-to-day battles. We need to take time out of the current noise and demands that are pressing against us and refresh our soul with a concerted focus on our dream of 'what could be'. This enables us to re-imagine all the possibilities, opportunities and benefits and remind ourselves of why we are persisting with our journey.

v. Our Internal Voice

External opposition, adverse events or critical voices barraging us are reasonably obvious obstacles. Sometimes, though, it's what's happening inside that creates barriers and limitations in our thinking and beliefs.

What we assume is an external obstacle can be an insidious, hidden internal voice that is slowly crippling our level of persistence. These voices can stem from our doubts and pre-existing negative thinking patterns. They can speak to us in numerous ways that produce fear, intimidation, anxiety and a poor self-image.

This internal critic can stop us if we have not developed our level of persistence enough to overcome it. For example, the thought that 'you are not good enough to be a leader' can echo through our mind and unconsciously permeate our thinking.

If we believe that thought, we will interpret every event in our life as confirmation. We will continue to gather information to prove our view is correct!

Until we address our thinking, we will primarily be trying to move past a boundary that we have set for ourselves—trying to escape from the very place we handcuffed ourselves to. It's an exhausting cycle, and eventually we run out of the energy to fight it—and give up.

We can't win in the environment outside us when we have not had victory over the environment inside us.

We can, however, learn to bring thoughts that oppose our success into submission, retaining only those that help us progress toward our goal.

---

*Everything you've ever wanted
is on the other side of fear.*
—George Addair

Jan was a fantastic human-resource coordinator in her job in community health services. Passionate about the industry, she had set herself on a path to reach management when she graduated from college. Years back, though, Jan had a bad experience as acting team leader for a couple of weeks, where undeservedly other staff had opposed her decision-making, disrespected her in a group meeting and raised issues against her with management. Even though this occurred eighteen years ago and all those staff had moved on, the experience left her believing she could never transition to a management role, despite consistently overachieving in all aspects of her work. When the department-manager role opened up, everyone assumed Jan would be the walk-in favourite.

But Jan believed a different story. She doubted her ability, didn't think anyone would listen to her as the manager, and was sure that many more qualified and capable people than herself would seek the job. Convinced she would not be successful, she didn't even apply, despite being asked to several times by senior directors.

Jan perceived that all her obstacles to moving forward were outside—the superior skills of other applicants, the potential negative response to her as manager—yet the biggest obstacles were inside her own thinking.

If we lack the persistence to move past our internally imposed boundaries, we are more likely to stop or give up on our journey.

vi. External voices

Generally speaking, there will always be more voices telling us to give up than to keep going.

If we're not careful, these negative voices speaking to us can start to become the dominant influence on us and our reference point to decide whether we persevere with our goal.

> *Don't let negative and toxic people rent space in your head. Raise the rent and kick them out!*
> —Robert Trew

Negative external voices can come from numerous sources:

- **The people affected by our stance.**

    Sometimes they may be attempting to silence or stop us because we are unsettling a situation they control or is benefitting them that will be affected if we bring change. It's in their best interests to stop us disturbing the status quo of the environment they are reaping a reward from and in their attempts to make us stop, these voices can become loud and aggressive.

- **Family, friends and colleagues,**

    The voice of our family, workmates and close friends can be extremely powerful. These groups often represent the closest, most consistent daily interactions we have, which means they can also be the most influential reference group we have.

    These groups often have their own particular culture, and if we step out of that culture to live by a different standard, this can create a reaction. They may be well intentioned or not, but sometimes family and friends like to remind us of all the reasons why our efforts are in vain, illogical, or could be put to better use elsewhere.

    While this feedback can be given out of concern, with our best interests at heart, it may still be a limiting force working against us.

    It's always wise to seek counsel from objective, trusted people. But ultimately, we need to follow the voice on the inside of our heart. In the end, it's our belief and conviction in our heart that will provide us with the fuel to power us forward in our level of persistence. If we feel like we are running a race because somebody told us to, we are less likely to persist.

Chapter Five – Persistence

Dave's friendship group, which had been thick as thieves since high school, were now all adults with families of their own. The 'boys' would typically gather on weekends for some serious sport watching and drinking. The boozy culture was part and parcel of their focus, and there was a strong expectation that participation in the drinks rituals was a part of the group's activities.

Which is why it made a big splash when at Saturday's session Dave, handed a beer, declined, declaring he was 'good, thanks'. At first, the group laughed it off, then realising he was serious asked him to explain himself.

Dave had committed to give up drinking, for no other reason than he felt he needed to for a season. He'd made a promise to his wife. Now, confronted with the full force of the group's pull back to the fold, he had to decide if he was going to renege.

Dave stuck to his guns, enduring some fairly harsh prods from some of his best friends, which agitated him and strained several relationships. 'What do they care if I drink or not?' he pondered? Some months later a friend who had had the strongest reaction confided to Dave that his stance challenged him, because he himself didn't think himself capable of making such a decision. When Dave displayed the personal leadership to step out of that culture, it inadvertently created conflict with others in the group, who felt much more comfortable if Dave were adhering to the status quo.

Sometimes as leaders, the greatest opponents to us continuing on our journey are those closest to us, who feel the most challenged if we are able to make it through.

CHAPTER SIX

Leading for Legacy

Legacy: Something transmitted by or received from an ancestor or predecessor or from the past

One of the ways our impact as a leader can be measured is through our ability to continue to influence the world after we have left it.

This impact defines our *leadership legacy*.

The harsh reality is that if we're not leading in a way that builds something that lasts, or that has a lasting impact, our leadership cannot impact people and our environment in an ongoing manner.

For many of us this reality can be a challenging concept because we are likely giving 100 per cent in what we're doing—and even producing excellent results. However, as leaders, we can be so focused on pushing forward today that we do not give much consideration to tomorrow.

The strength of what we build as a leader will ultimately be proven by how long it lasts. A house built using sound design principles, tested construction techniques and quality materials, under direction from a wise master builder, will last many generations. A house built by shortcutting any of these essential elements is unlikely to last for the long term.

> *Even though our time in this life is*
> *temporary, if we live well enough,*
> *our legacy will last forever.*
> —Idowu Koyenikan

History is littered with people who rose to fame, gained power, pioneered projects or created significant initiatives. However, for all but a relatively small percentage, their leadership impact is here today and gone tomorrow. The blueprint of how they operated never defined or communicated, and therefore never emulated by others.

During the term of our leadership, we may enjoy popularity, power, achievements, prestige and position. However, these can be a superficial and temporary byproduct that lasts only for a brief time. A shooting star that makes a brilliant, high-profile impact on the night sky is gone just as quickly as it came, its evidence of ever being a highlight on the landscape erased.

Unless we build accurately and invest our lives wisely, our leadership endeavours can be just as fleeting as the shooting star.

Present-Focused Leadership

If we invest our life into a cause we believe in, a family we love or an enterprise we own, we will no doubt have sacrificed for it.

What a tragedy if everything we have toiled for and built over our leadership tenure is quickly eradicated when we step out of our leadership role. This scenario is similar to the multitowered sandcastle that is meticulously and painstakingly sculpted at the beach over the entire hot summer day, only to be washed away by the incoming tide at sunset. Of all the effort, energy and skill that went into creating that castle, causing it to rise out of the beach sand, and as good as the quality was, the environment quickly reduces it to nothing. It bears no evidence that it ever even existed.

> *The great use of life is to spend it*
> *for something that will outlast it.*
> —William James

To spend our life building something, only to have it reduced to nothing, is heartbreaking. Yet this is a typical pattern of occurrence amongst many people functioning in leadership roles today.

Why does this happen? And how can we prevent it?

The Limitations of Succession Planning

When we start to discuss the topic of leadership continuity, the common turn of phrase in a company setting is 'succession planning'.

Succession planning is the appointment and promotion of a suitably qualified and experienced person to fill a leadership role that has been vacated. [50]

The problem with relying solely on 'succession planning' to hand down a leadership role is that it can tend to place an overly dominant focus on a candidate's skill and ability, but overlook the connection and commitment to the current leader's vision, purpose, principles and priorities.

Ed Catmull is the co-founder of Pixar and president of Walt Disney Animation Studios, responsible for creating movies such as *Toy Story*. Its feature films have earnt approximately $14 billion at the worldwide box office. Ed describes the limitations of succession planning when he says that 'everybody talks about succession planning because of its importance, but to me the issue that's missed is cultural succession. You have to make sure the next level down understands what the actual values are. For example, Walt Disney was driven by technological change and he brought that energy into the company. But after he died, the people left didn't fully understand how he thought. Thus, the value wasn't passed on and it fell away from the company. It didn't come back until Walt's nephew, Roy Disney Jr, used his authority to reintroduce the concept. Today, much of our senior leadership's time is spent making sure our values are deeply embedded at every level of our organisation. It is very challenging—but necessary for us to continue making great movies'.[51]

When the approach to succession planning emphasizes the successor's individual capabilities and previous achievements, that successor may introduce a different agenda and values. When this happens, the new leader begins to alter the DNA of the established culture. In those situations where the culture needs changing, this is a healthy practice. But where past success has been the result of the forefather's fundamental blueprint, principles and focus, the new leader can start to undermine the foundation.

To ensure a more accurate model of leadership continuity and handover, we must look away from succession planning to a different concept: 'legacy transfer'. Legacy transfer can occur in a family, workplace, community or organisational setting.

The Concept of Legacy Transfer

Legacy is what the pioneer of one generation labours for, builds and establishes, then strategically sows into and passes to the next generation. The content of this transfer is not so much focused on possessions, but on the personal internal dynamics, priorities, values, victories and lessons carried by the forefather.

Legacy transfer is different than the passing on of money and property, often associated with the term 'inheritance'.

> *The greatest legacy one can pass on to one's children and grandchildren is not money or other material things accumulated in one's life, but rather a legacy of character and faith.*
> —Billy Graham

The difference between legacy and inheritance is that the transfer of legacy is implicitly linked to the fulfilment of the mandate of the predecessor's mission. The transfer's purpose is to enable a continuation of the initial leader's journey, using the same pattern of operating. In effect, recipients of legacy transfer pick up and progress the previous generation's assignment by building on the existing platform, using the same principles, albeit with their particular personality and style.

> *Legacy is not leaving something for people, it's leaving something in people.*
> —Peter Strople

Legacy transfer is made possible by the heart connection and alignment of lives between one generation and another. It is not merely reshuffling names and positions on an organisational chart.

It is the deep-seated heart connection between two or more generations that allows the transfer of the dreams, stature, dynamics, purpose, vision and passion of the founding leader. Relationship is the supply line to resource this connection. It is the only vehicle for legacy transfer.

If we do not build according to the principle of legacy transfer, all of our energy and work as leaders can disappear at the passing of the baton, just like the sandcastle on the beach.

A construction company that started as a one-man operation in 1984 had grown to be the contractor of choice for the state's biggest construction projects.

It had grown off the back of the hard word and courage of its owner and operator, Harry. Harry's 'strategic plan' for success was simple: 'work hard, hire good people, support each other'. And that was as complex as he made the strategy.

Harry developed a loyal band of close-knit supervisors and tradespeople, who were something of an extended family. They were dedicated to working hard for Harry, who rewarded them with years of constant employment. Harry paid generously, expecting a suitable return, and it was this goodwill, trust and mutual respect that epitomized the organisation's culture. Harry never checked the hours his team told him they worked, and they never shortchanged him with a half-hearted effort.

Harry, though, a huge brute of a man, had pushed his body to its physical limits with years of backbreaking labour, and had reached the age where now even office work was a challenge. He needed to step away and find a replacement. Unsure of how to create a handover plan, Harry was referred to a corporate consultant, who advised him of their recruitment strategy—to find the brightest and sharpest replacement CEO.

Harry felt he had invested too much into the business and his team to risk making a poor decision on his own. Not knowing anything about succession plans, he took the consultant's advice. Four months later they delivered their best candidate. Sean—young, sharp, well educated—had a history of increasing profit at a number of previous companies and came highly recommended. Over several meetings with Harry, Sean outlined his plan for the future. Harry handed over the reins to Sean, confident his company was in good hands.

However, months later, word began to filter back to Harry of unrest in the workforce. Some top employees were raising concerns. They informed Harry that Sean had implemented a cumbersome start-time card clock to check whether staff were arriving late; in order to ensure staff weren't stealing, he had added clauses to employment contracts to deduct pay from workers if equipment went missing, and he had banned the legendary Friday post-work barbecues. These all struck at the organisation-wide environment of trust and relationship.

It soon became clear that Sean had a very different approach to dealing with people and running the company. For instance, Harry believed the free weekly barbecues were a healthy reward for the team's hard work. He also knew the niggles and issues that occur between workers could be ironed out over a meal and a drink. Stamped out early, these issues didn't linger and affect output.

Upon reflection, Harry had buyer's remorse. He realised that some of the loyal long-term foundational members of his 'family', who didn't have formal qualifications but had sweat and blood invested in the company, who carried the heartbeat of his values, would have been a better choice to continue his legacy than someone imported in from outside. If this trend continued, in just a few short months, the culture and ethos Harry had spent a lifetime developing could soon be wiped away.

Harry is now in the process of wrestling back control of the company and is committed to handing the reins to one of 'his' people, not an outsider who doesn't understand the core values that made the company so successful.

As leaders, we can't pass on our work to just anyone and expect it to continue the way we want. If we want the culture and modus operandi of what we built to continue after we're gone, we need well in advance to prepare people to carry our legacy.

The Mindset of a Legacy Leader

As we grow as a legacy leader, our concept of success becomes *less about our achievements, and more about being able to reproduce ourselves in the hearts and minds of another generation* so our work can continue after we've gone. Establishing the pattern of our approach in others becomes a priority.

As this revelation deepens in us, we start to operate with a 'building' mentality to establish permanence, rather than a 'performance' mentality to seek success and meet temporary needs. Results may be slower and more incremental, but they are ultimately more sustainable than a fast-paced, quick-results approach. Our focus as a legacy leader becomes about building well, more than achieving quickly, to ensure long-term results as opposed to short-term accolades.

> *The final test of a leader is that he leaves behind him, in other men, the conviction and the will to carry on.*
> —Walter Lippman

There is no point in striving and pushing as a leader all the days of our life, only to reach the eleventh hour and very twilight of our time to suddenly start searching for someone to take over. By then, it's too late.

To become an effective legacy leader, we need to start with the last day of our leadership journey in mind, and work backward from that point to today. That means we need to ask ourselves early on in our leadership journey: 'How is what I am building going to last into the future? . . . Who will carry on my work to fulfil the assignment? . . . What do the people connected with me need to equip and empower them so they can propagate the pattern with others into the future?'

When we start to build for longevity, not just results, we begin to adjust our leadership mentality accordingly. We start to operate with the realisation that our time is finite. And as good, high-achieving and talented as we may be, all our work will ultimately simply end with us if we have not prepared well.

A 4 x 100-metre relay race is won using four different runners. In the context of legacy transfer, each baton change represents another generation. As legacy leaders, we are not so worried about running the fastest leg; we are more concerned about the baton reaching the finishing line. Equipping and preparing the other runners in our team to complete their leg of the race becomes as big a priority as our performance.

Our concern is more focused on ensuring that we will finish the race. The realisation that we cannot impact the next generation when we are gone, only while we are here, develops within us an increasing urgency to connect with and train others, knowing that the future success of our work lies with them.

When we transition in our thinking towards legacy, we will start to focus on connecting with and developing those who are potential 'carriers' of our assignment for tomorrow. We won't see those around us anymore as just another family member, employee or group member, but we start to see them as a potential recipient who can continue our journey into the future. By extension, we recognise that they will be the ones who will, in turn, connect with, shape and impart this legacy to the next generation again. As individuals, we can be stopped by the reality of the number of days in our life, but if we build as legacy leaders, our message, vision and purpose can become everlasting.

The function of leadership is to produce more leaders, not more followers.
—Ralph Nader

When our assignment, vision and values start to be captured by the next generation, and we start to share the same dream in our heart, we have multiple generations running with the same mission and passion, and that starts to become a picture of legacy transfer. If we can achieve this as long before our departure as possible, then we can be confident of our legacy continuing.

Transferring to the Next Generation

Our ability and capacity to connect with and train the next generation is essential. If there is no connection, there can be no transfer.

No matter what our personality, or our previous role models in this regard, we must develop the relational dynamics to bridge the gap to the next generation.

To achieve this, we may have to break out of our own self. If we are not accustomed to engaging, relating and connecting, this may be a completely foreign concept to us. However, our independent, self-contained approach may be the stumbling block to reaching the hearts and minds of the next generation, and this is what can stop our legacy from being transferred.

Strategically Shaping the Next Generation

We do not want to leave the transfer of legacy to chance. While some people may appear more likely candidates to run with our assignment into the future, it is most likely that even these will need some input, realignment and moulding to enable them to receive legacy accurately.

That's why we need a proactive and strategic approach to preparing those who may take the baton from us, to align them well with our assignment so they can continue the race well. If we adopt a relational approach with a focus on communication and a progressively deepening level of transparency, those around us can start to gain key insights into our mindset, values, priorities and vision for the future. Understanding more about us in this way allows them the opportunity to become tuned in to our frequency. This process requires us as leaders to be the instigators of reaching out in an open, engaging and consistent approach to make a genuine heart connection.

We need to be wise about recognising, who is responding to us. We don't want to be chasing after people if they are not interested in anything to do with us or our goals. We also cannot assume that those who are close to us geographically, who see us regularly or who have been with us for a long time are closely aligned to us in their heart. We may presume that they are connected in and committed, yet they may have a very different agenda, approach and ambition than ours. If we are not discerning of where people are, we can be left shocked, and our work damaged when they eventually leave or go in another direction.

Obstacles to Connecting with the Next Generation

Knowing that our connection with the next generation is crucial for legacy transfer, how will we move past the internal obstacles that can limit us from connecting with them? As leaders for legacy, we are responsible for reaching them, not vice versa.

Identifying these obstacles is a good starting point, and common ones can include:

1. Being so consumed with our performance and achievements we don't develop or prepare anyone around us

2. Seeing ourselves as 'workers' but not 'trainers or mentors'—just producers, not suppliers

3. Having a fear of technology and equipment that we do not understand but which the next generation grasps; the potential for a sense of inferiority or intimidation this fear creates in us

4. Holding a preconceived idea that they would not be interested in continuing our journey, but would only want to start their own, self-focused venture

5. Relying on holding a position of authority as the basis for connection with others, where traditionally being the 'senior', in age or position, was enough to gain respect

6. Lacking the communication and relationship–building skills to engage and connect with others

Once we identify these obstacles (you may find others), we can start developing a plan to overcome them so they do not remain a barrier to bridging the generation gap.

Keys for Building Legacy Transfer

We can begin to transition into a legacy leader by incorporating several key principles into our leadership approach. Six of these keys are below:

i. Adopt a building, not performance, mentality

Everyone loves results, and as leaders we should always have a healthy regard for achievement. But we also need to be wary of pursuing short-term success at the expense of building solid foundations. Achievement and performance cannot be the only measures we use to gauge the quality of our progress. A first place, highest attendance or greatest profit today, is not an indicator of sustained success and impact tomorrow.

Legacy leaders function with a *building* mentality, not just a *results* mentality.

> *We cannot always build the future for our youth,*
> *but we can always build our youth for the future.*
> —Franklin D. Roosevelt

In a well-constructed 100-storey skyscraper, the foundations must drive deep into the earth, providing the strength required to support the weight of the structure. Foundational work takes time. At first, there is little visible progress, and rarely are there flashy features to be seen, despite the months, even years, of hard preparation work. But at an appointed time, when the foundations are established and the construction starts to rise above the ground floor, a very visible, strong, lasting building is established on this platform. As leaders, we can build superficially for a quick result, but we can't build anything of significance or durability unless we establish the foundations accurately.

There are no shortcuts to creating a durable generational work.

ii. Build people, not systems

Programs can be imported, rules can be applied, policies implemented and systems established, but the most valuable asset to us as leaders is great people. That's why when we are leading with a view to legacy transfer, we operate with a focus on building people, not systems, because we understand that in the end, it will be people that ultimately carry the heart and energy of our vision, not a program or a policy. Software can be installed out of a box, and procedures can be cut and pasted from the internet, but these things won't carry our purpose forward when we're gone. It's the people we have built up and transferred legacy to that will be behind the wheel, driving the passion of our values forward into the future.

That's why we must always value the opportunity to develop, impart to and train those connected to us, even though our investment can take months, years or even decades to see a return. Our focus needs to be on equipping and upgrading people's skill, understanding, capacity and effectiveness, constantly sowing the seed of our vision into the hearts and minds of others and creating an environment where they can *buy in* and take ownership of it.

We realise that the strength of our people will ensure our ongoing success and the sustainability of our vision.

Our future leaders are ultimately our entire future.

Lydia had built her IT service business from the garage of her parents' house, to the prime-time retail strip of her city. She employed twenty staff, had gained numerous high-paying contracts and was now a competitor to some of the biggest international service centres. The key to Lydia's success was her painstaking work in customising her cutting-edge systems and software that coordinated customer-service requests and status reports on individual jobs, itemised invoicing coordinated with technicians' work and automated email to customers and suppliers. This customized software made the operation extremely efficient. She was proud of what she had created and would often boast that her systems were so good 'this place could run itself'; her connection to her creations was so strong she often called her integration and interface software 'my babies'.

Drawing the attention of international competitors, Lydia was actually presented a lucrative offer to buy her out, including all her patented integrations in her systems. Thinking it was a deal she couldn't pass up, she accepted and walked away from the business to retire, thrilled that her years of innovative and painstaking work were going to be replicated in a major corporation with outlets all over the globe.

Lydia was wrong, though. From her contacts still in the business, she was shocked to learn three months later that none of her processes or systems had been carried over, but were simply discarded and replaced by the new owner. They had bought her out purely to maintain their market advantage, which she was encroaching upon, so they simply introduced their own systems into their business and hers were never seen again.

As Lydia had signed over all intellectual property, it meant she could never even replicate what she had created and would certainly never be able to use it again. It was effectively lost to the world forever.

Lydia's business was built on systems and processes, but these things in and of themselves cannot carry legacy. They can be replaced or discarded. Ultimately, our legacy can only be carried on in people.

iii. Build according to principles, not popularity.

Whether it's a family, political party, business or community group, as legacy leaders we need to establish what our foundational nonnegotiable core values and principles are, set them in stone and then build upon them. If these are not clear, the next generation will compromise them.

Avoid popularity.
It has many snares and no real benefit.
—William Penn

While the temptation to be popular is enticing, popularity is not an achievable or sustainable principle to build upon. In construction terms, a cornerstone is the point of the structure that all other stones are laid in reference to: it orients the entire building in a specific direction upon which the rest of a structure is built. Imagine the chaos if—depending on the popular opinion of those involved or of casual outside observers who had an opinion to offer—the cornerstone of a building under construction moved every day. The builder and tradespeople would constantly be tearing down and redoing work completed the previous day to cater to the new reference point. They would simply never be able to build the house to completion, never finish it for the intended purpose.

What is popular one day is not always so the next. So popularity is not a relevant cornerstone to build anything on.

When we lead according to the permanency of principles, we will yield far better long-term outcomes than building by ever-changing popular opinion.

Principles and values are the bedrock of individual, family or organisation life. If these are clearly established, promoted and modelled by us as leaders, it provides a clear reference point in our culture and a pathway for others to follow and be aligned with.

iv. **Build on character, not personality or talent.**

Personality is temporary and talent skin deep, but character is permanent—it goes right to the bone.

If we're building for the future, we need to be more focused on character than skills or charisma.

The strong, talented, loud, magnetic personality may appear superficially to be a natural 'leader'—an obvious choice. But if we are looking for suitable recipients of the legacy-transfer mantle, we are in many ways actually looking for empty vessels.

If they are unwilling to let go of their things to carry ours, someone full of personality, abilities, confidence and plans may not have any room left to take on our values or mission.

If our focus is on achieving results quickly, we are more likely to promote talented individuals who can produce good results. However, as legacy leaders, we are looking to build well, build strong and build for the future, so we are less focused on the immediate 'star', more focused on those with enduring internal qualities.

Character is more important than talent.
—Edwin Louis Cole

Strong personalities oozing talent and capabilities can potentially be great legacy carriers if they are well aligned with our heart and mission. If not, they can be trouble. People can be talented and influential, with strong ambition, but not connected to us or our purpose. If we promote that person as the headline act, if we're not careful, we can find ourselves planning around their needs rather than our collective vision. Particularly in community groups, political parties and networks that operate more so by loyalties and alliances than a clear chain of command.

In these environments a charismatic leader may attract 'protégés' from within the group who align with their own values rather than those of the founder or leader. The divergence creates a division in the camp, as it effectively creates two competing sets of leadership values, approaches and energies. This results in several issues:

1. The charismatic leader may leave, taking a group of followers out the door. That can leave a giant-sized hole in the foundation of our work, a tremendous setback.

2. Or given the charismatic leader's leverage, he or she can become too 'big' to bring into line, the potential cost of the charismatic leader's reaction is too damaging. Then we have effectively allowed our work to be taken over.

3. We can be compromised in our ability to lead, as to gain the acceptance of the influential pseudo leader (with followers), we can be forced to consult on decision-making. We are effectively held to ransom with the threat of a revolt or a walkout.

When we build on character, we look for those whose hearts are for us, demonstrate humility towards us, are coachable, loyal and prepared to surrender their ambition to take up our goals. These are the ones who will carry our assignment into the future. They may not immediately present with these characteristics, but as we continue to reach out and connect with them, we can more easily identify them as they progress on this journey and align with us.

v. **Build for the collective objective, not individual potential**

While the common, popular theme of *reaching your potential* is empowering and positive, when we look at it within a broader movement, it needs some re-messaging.

As leaders, we don't want to necessarily encourage people to use their talents as a personal platform to highlight themselves.

In sports, being named the league top scorer is a tremendous personal accolade, but what does it matter if it comes at the expense of the team's success? In the workplace, the prestige of leading the advertising department in sales by resorting to cutting across your team members' accounts is ultimately counterproductive for the organisation. A dad who spends countless hours at home restoring a 1967 Chevrolet Chevelle Classic to pristine condition, becoming the star of the car club, in the process may sacrifice quality relationships with his family. The reality is that while 'being all you can be' is a healthy aspirational goal, at some stage personal sacrifice is also required to achieve collective success.

Our leadership approach needs to create a healthy balance between individual personal development and the contribution to our shared vision and goals. Otherwise, there is always a tension between individuals reaching for *their* goals, and the group reaching for the *collective* goal.

As we continue to promote the priority of the 'team', we create a culture where individuals realise it's not about 'them', it's about 'us'.

Noah was the coordinator of a community youth group of around thirty kids aged fourteen to nineteen. Their mandate was to provide growth opportunities for young people in a positive environment. One department, the music team, rehearsed each week and played for free at community events, shopping malls and gatherings. The band was an effective way for young people to apply their passion for music, learn about being part of a team, make social connections and contribute to their local community.

Noah had appointed Amelia as the band leader, as Amelia was closely aligned to the goals and aims of the youth group.

She respected Noah, related well to people in the group and represented him and the group well in public settings. Alexander and Olivia were a couple who were extremely talented musically and long-time members of the band, with lots of community connections to open opportunities for the band to perform. They seemed on the surface an obvious replacement to take on the leadership and were pushing hard to take on the coordinator's role as Amelia had indicated she was moving away for study.

Noah, however, was uncomfortable at the idea of handing over the role to them. Despite their musical gifting, they were disconnected from the vision of the youth group, had at times used the band as an opportunity to promote themselves rather than the group, had been critical of Amelia's leadership, were often distant from Noah relationally, and had a history of conflict with members of the group. He wasn't sure they would be a good influence on the band members and was concerned the music program may become a 'closed shop' to his input if Alexander and Olivia created a division between 'their music program' and the rest of the youth group.

Noah appointed Mason as Amelia's replacement. Mason, had been in the youth group for many years. He had only average music ability, but had proven his commitment to the vision of the youth group, was very open to input from Noah and had proven himself a real servant of the youth groups activities.

Noah's wise choice was based on who would best move forward the collective success of the group and keep it aligned to the overarching vision, not who was most talented. His choice was vindicated when Alexander and Olivia left the area to lead another community-youth-group music program, which soon after reported high levels of internal conflict and division that effectively saw the group and program cease to function.

vi. Build deep, not wide

We don't need multitudes to hand the baton over to; we only need one.

It is important that we focus on building deep, strong connections, possibly with just a few, rather than building shallow and superficial connections with a multitude, because numbers have never been a good indicator of the continuation of legacy.

We are better off prioritising our time with a few who are aligning accurately with our message and lifestyle, as these will represent us and continue our work more faithfully than a crowd who never really connected with us or caught what was in our hearts.

The Defining Characteristics of an Accurate Legacy Recipient

In essence, we are looking for the next runner in the race to receive the baton and carry legacy for the subsequent leg in the race.

Our assessment is crucial. Selecting the wrong person jeopardises the effectiveness of our work into successive generations. The correct choice will see our work continue to gather momentum and multiply.

While there are never any cast-iron rules or formulas to choose by, there is an essential set of qualities we can reference that will provide us with a strong framework for our selection process. These are also the qualities we ourselves must demonstrate if we are to carry another person's legacy forward.

i. Honouring the current leadership

If the protégé does not honour the mentor, legacy cannot be imparted. Honour is the vehicle through which information, understanding and spirit are transferred. If a high achiever or the best performer has no regard for the leader, that person can receive nothing of the leader's tangible or intangible qualities and dynamics.

To honour someone simply means to treat a person or regard that person with special attention and respect.[52]

To honour the patriarch or matriarch of a family or the head of a business or political party in no way means we believe he or she is perfect and has made no mistakes. On the contrary, it means we afford respect and recognition for the stature they carry, the character they display, the achievements they've attained and the sacrifice they've incurred. Legacy recipients understand they are standing on the shoulders of forefathers and as such value them and the foundations they laid. Honouring means greatly valuing. With humility we draw what they carry into our own lives, and in certain cases, we are prepared to prioritise our life plan to continue what they developed.

Aiden was the sole owner of a small manufacturing business that made specialised plastic containers for offshore oil and gas operations. He had two key managers, Owen and Mila. Owen, the operations manager, was responsible for rostering staff, maintaining factory machinery and other equipment and transporting products. Mila was the corporate manager, responsible for financial activities, human resources and health and safety. She was, not incidentally, also Aiden's daughter.

Aiden's company had recently won two new contracts that would require them to add plant, equipment and staff. It also meant a revised business hierarchy that would need to introduce a second in charge to Aiden. He knew this role was effectively an apprenticeship to take over the business when he eventually stepped into retirement.

Having decided to keep the appointment internal, he would soon have to select between Mila and Owen who had both indicated an eagerness to carry on the business.

Mila (highly intelligent, strong, extremely capable) had an academic background in business and manufacturing. Owen had arrived at the plant as a young man before learning the ropes and risen through the ranks. He was a very quick learner, extremely respectful of Aiden, who was something of a role model and mentor for him. He was always grateful for the assistance and opportunity Aiden provided. As such, he worked hard and always made room for Aiden's input. He spoke his mind to Aiden, stating if he disagreed with a proposal—however, would support Aiden wholeheartedly once he made a decision.

Aiden loved Mila as any father loved his daughter, but he also saw her blind spots and weaknesses, which raised red flags about her suitability for the role. Feeling many of her ideas were superior to Aiden's, Mila frequently dismissed him when he tried to provide insight or an experienced view. Aiden acknowledged the business had scope for expansion, but Mila's demanding attitude often felt more like a hostile takeover. She would frequently act against his directions. As his daughter, she felt entitled to boss her dad around. Aiden

Chapter Six – Leading for Legacy

wondered, 'If Mila acts like that now, what's she going to do if she has even more authority?'

Aiden had a few business non-negotiables in place, such as the terms of his payment to suppliers, which he insisted be done at the end of every month.

Mila had long argued to implement an alternative method—in which payment would be made prior to receiving the product, at the same time qualifying Aiden's company for discounted pricing. Owen tried this system before—nearly going bankrupt, as the suppliers consistently double billed him because of their lack of administrative ability to keep track of upfront payments.

But Mila refused to listen and often spoke of 'putting it in place as soon as he wasn't looking'.

Aiden knew the potential for conflict in the family if he appointed Owen over Mila, but despite this, he was not prepared to jeopardise the future of his business. He duly appointed Owen, based on his protégé's capabilities in part but largely because of his own confidence that Owen would work collaboratively with him, and together they would provide a united, stable front to the operation.

As leaders in our family, community group or workplace, if our successor does not display a level of honour toward us, a capacity to work in agreement with us and a respect for the foundation we built laboriously, we cannot expect legacy to be transferred well to the next generation.

ii. **Representing the leader accurately**

Representing a leader accurately is not about trying to create copycats, clones or yes-men. People's individual identities will always have their own flavour. It does mean, however, that potential legacy recipients can represent the ethos, heart, values and priorities of the forefather accurately.

Mary and Barry's parents had a healthy family tradition of a Sunday-night meal to connect, share, debrief and laugh together. A time of real family bonding. As a son and daughter who had internalized the value of prioritising these dinners, they replicated the tradition by continuing to meet when their parents passed away.

Aligning with their parents' mentality, behaviour, priorities and values in this instance and applying the same practice in their own homes, they carried on the legacy of the family culture their mum and dad had established, and then passed it onto their children as well.

As a director in an organisation that consulted on environmental sustainability, Lance modelled an approach to working through conflict constructively with the two managers who reported to him, Tim and Anne. Tim had adopted Lance's leadership approach with his team, developing great skills in unpacking and resolving conflict in a healthy manner . But despite Lance's coaching, Anne handled conflict very differently. She treated any sign of disagreement as a personal attack she needed to defend herself against, using coercion, legal technicalities and a quick rallying of allies to support her view.

Complaints from her staff about her style were high, while Tim's group had not raised an issue with him for as long as Lance could remember. Lance knew that if Anne were to assume his role as the department leader, then the nature and character of the entire department would change very quickly, for the worse.

Legacy recipients in any domain, be it family, work or community, must not introduce a dynamic that is inconsistent with the leader's modus operandi. If people are not well connected to the leader relationally, it's unlikely they will be able to accurately continue the work in the vein it was started.

iii. Open to and seeking input from the founder

With splinters, sharp edges, knots and irregular shapes the rough-sawn tree trunk enters the timber mill. Still, it emerges on the other side as a functional, practical piece of timber capable of being used for its intended function. While many people have talents, potential and capability, it is also normal for us all to need some work in the timber mill, to develop character, add capacity, sand down the rough edges and adjust a few mentalities. People rarely arrive fully prepared, trained, and ready to go.

What you didn't know in the story above is that when Tim commenced his job ten years prior, he was just like Anne. But Tim had acknowledged to Lance that he feared and hated conflict, reacted poorly to it, and needed help to handle it. Lance's input had transformed Tim's whole approach. As a result of being open to the input of another leader ahead of him, he became a significantly improved leader in his own right.

When someone allows you into their life, letting you get close enough to impart into them and address those areas that need maturing, that person is likely most qualified to receive the legacy. In the above example, that's Tim, not Anne.

When we position ourselves to receive discipline, correction and input because we value what someone carries and trust that person to help us in our journey, we are setting ourselves up for legacy transfer. We see it more as a personal relationship than just a business transaction.

We may even appoint such a person as the primary source of input to our life, on all matters—becoming our reference point, our cornerstone to build on. Rather than 'shopping around' to find someone's opinion to justify or approve what we have already decided to do, we set aside a special place in our life for this person's input and guidance to direct us.

People who are 'above' being trained, feel they are already 'qualified' or are unwilling to acknowledge their need for further development largely disqualify themselves, as unsuitable to take the baton from the leader into the next generation. If they are not willing to align their life and values with the leader, how can they represent them or their work accurately into the future?

---

*Never make someone a priority
when they only see you as an option.*
—Mary Mihalic

---

iv. **Committed to continuing the work of the leader**

Legacy transfer is about receiving the mandate and dynamics to continue to progress an established purpose, vision and work of a predecessor with a specific direction and destination in mind.

Accurate legacy recipients do not look for an opportunity to start their own work, but they have reached a point where the prior leader's assignment has become their assignment. They are now two entities working toward the same goal and beating with the same heart. They are wanting to carry on what has already been established, taking the work or cause further. They are not looking for a new fad—do not want to start their own project by abandoning the previous foundations, sacrifices and progress made by the previous leader.

They don't see serving the prior leader's goals as a substitute or second-best option; it is a pursuit and an environment that brings them total satisfaction and fulfillment. They are not looking for where else they can apply their talent but invest their energy, efforts and sacrifice into the leader's work.

The concept of legacy transfer does not operate on the currency of good leaders, who may be able just to lead *something* to *somewhere*. It operates on the currency of followers connected to the leader, who can work according to the forefather's values and intended destination. That means they first have to be good carriers of the work, already locked into the existing assignment. Receivers of legacy must be internally committed to the purpose of the predecessor and have received a dimension of what they carry to continue to run the race.

v. Tried and tested

Just because someone has been around for a long time doesn't mean they are qualified to take on a leadership mantle. Nor does it mean that new arrivals cannot become leaders. However, when someone has been through a mixture of ups and downs, trials and tests, conflict, disappointment, victories, offence, discipline, correction and successes and still remains connected to the leader and on the job, it provides a fairly good indicator they are in it for the long haul. This length of tenure also provides the opportunity to develop a much clearer picture of what's really inside that person. This clarity is really gained only through an extended window of time, observing through a variety of situations.

A relatively new member to a team who performs well and says all the right things may still have some unrevealed and unhealthy attitudes or agendas under the surface. These character qualities will perhaps only be exposed over time as the environment presents challenges, they experience unmet expectations or relationships are tested.

---

*Endurance is a much better test of character
than heroism, however noble.*
—John Lubbock

How do they respond when they are promoted? Or challenged about a behaviour? Or don't get what they want? Or when they are held accountable?

It's possible to gain a certain perspective of someone's character and commitment after walking with them for a year, but there is a much deeper understanding after walking with that person for twenty years. We must not hasten to transfer legacy to those who are unproven or untested in their ability to stay in relationship with us through the rigours of life's journey.

If people have negative traits, if they react poorly to the above scenarios, they should not be ruled out as potential legacy transfer recipients, by any means. It's better to know someone's strengths and weaknesses, rather than just strengths. It simply allows the leader to be more aware of their level of maturity and character and to put a plan into place to help them grow in these areas.

'Better the devil you know' is an apt sentiment in this case. When others are transparent and open with the leader about how they feel or what they are struggling with, it allows a greater level of trust and confidence. It's the hidden skeletons lurking in the closet of people's character and makeup that have the potential to do the greatest damage, not the weaknesses that are openly placed on the table.

> *Transparency is the currency of trust.*
> —Christopher S. Penn

Creating Future Leaders

As leaders, we need to continue to encourage, support and invest in people who are letting their guard down and being real with us. These are the ones we can establish genuine heart connections with, grow with. The shiny, always smiling, well-dressed person who presents well, but never really lets us see what's going on in the inside, is possibly the one we need be a little more cautious of.

Creating a metal of great strength requires the addition of carbon combined with a 'transformational hardening' process, exposing the steel to severe heating and cooling to reduce its brittleness and increase its toughness. After this treatment, the metalworker is confident he has a quality product.

We cannot choose untested people to carry our work. We cannot build our future on material that has not been pressure tested. As leaders, we can 'manufacture' our form of heat and pressure testing that similarly combines 'carbon content' (our input and mentoring) with 'heat treatment' (the challenges of circumstances).

Choose those people who have the scars and length of tenure to prove they have been toughened through trial and pressure, and are still standing with us, refined, moulded and committed to our cause.

CHAPTER SEVEN
Selfless Service

Service: The action of helping or doing work for someone
Selfless: Concerned more with the needs and wishes of others than with one's own; unselfish

A young, eager member of a church felt a calling to become more involved in the outreach work of the church.

He presented himself to the senior pastor and announced he was 'ready' to begin his preaching career on the big stage to big crowds.

'Oh, so you're ready to start serving in the church?' asked the senior pastor. 'That's great! We've been looking for someone to clean the toilets'.

Welcome to the journey of selfless service. Where our ego and ambition is checked at the door as we apply our efforts to a vision greater than ourselves in pursuit of outcomes that benefit others.

Where we voluntarily choose to serve another person or cause, not our own needs and wants.

An inspiring picture of a lifestyle of selfless service is seen in the scenario of the low-income single parent who may be working numerous jobs to make ends meet and provide for the children, while likely being consumed with managing the daily logistical demands of their care, schooling and activities. Meeting these burdens has meant they long ago surrendered their ambitions and preferences to focus their efforts on ensuring their kids have enough. We'll likely never see such a person featured in a celebrity magazine, speak at a business seminar or appear on a prime-time TV talk show. But this is someone who has accessed and is living in a dimension of selfless service that epitomises this leadership characteristic.

There are two types of service:
1. self-service
2. service to others

To do well for our self is commendable. To serve others and assist in their success is exemplary.

Service of others means we *choose* to place someone else's needs and priorities ahead of our own. It is generated by care, concern and love for others. If we love someone, we'll serve that person. If we only love ourself, we'll only serve ourself. When we operate in the dimension of selfless service, our perspective on our life's purpose turns away from our own needs and towards the needs of others.

The purpose of human life is to serve, and to show compassion and the will to help others.
—Albert Schweitzer

Selfless service is fuelled by our internal motivation, not external rewards.

When we are service-focused, our leadership is not characterised by what we feel we are entitled to or by our expectation to be served in return; instead, we are powered by a passion for giving what we can and sowing into others.

> *Leadership is service, not position.*
> —Tim Fargo

The Foundations of Service

The words *slave, servant and service* derive from the same original Hebrew word, implying both 'action' and 'obedience'. Servants essentially belonged to someone. They were not their own master. Similarly, when we choose to serve someone else or their purpose, it can mean we surrender our right to serve ourself and assume the responsibility to serve someone or something else.[53]

During the Siege of Leningrad in September 1941, German forces choked the food supply to the two million residents of the city.

A group of Russian scientists and botanists at the Institute of Plant Industry barricaded themselves inside their secret vault in Leningrad to protect the 370,000 seeds, the greatest collection in the world, from both hungry Soviet citizens and the German army.

It was so important to them to conserve the world's food diversity and future agricultural produce they chose to starve to death rather than consume the seeds they were guarding for a postwar world.

One of the scientists is quoted as saying, 'Saving those seeds for future generations and helping the world recover after war was more important than a single person's comfort'.

These men put humankind ahead of their own personal lives, to demonstrate the greatest act of service imaginable.[54]

The Heart of a Servant

Service, primarily, is an attitude.

To serve others requires humility, surrender and deference in our heart. In effect, we lay down our own needs and ambitions to help fulfil someone else's. We lead by literally taking the shirt off our own back to provide for someone without.

The Community Development team of the local municipality conducted frequent community consultations on a number of issues ranging from sporting infrastructure, streetscapes and programs.

Zoe, the manager of the Community Development team, attended meetings with two staff members, Claire and Chris. Their approach to these meetings was strikingly different.

Claire would arrive right before the session started, typically complaining how this was another ruined night of her social life, before heading straight to the complimentary drinks-and-snacks table to make a coffee and search for the best remaining deserts; then she would proceed to sit by herself, often chewing and drinking even through Zoe's introductions and opening remarks. She spoke only if she had a presentation to make, in which case would simply demand, 'Where's the pointer?' (for the slides she was speaking about) and hurry out the door to her car as soon as the session was over.

Chris, however, would volunteer to pick up the catering on his way to the venue and ensure he arrived at least half an hour early to set up the projector and laptop for Zoe and Claire, making sure it was working OK. He would take the sweets tray around to the participants when they arrived and offer to get them drinks. Once the meting started, he was a careful listener, taking notes, and would chase up some information if Zoe didn't have an answer to a question.

After the meeting Chris would chat with community members, then pack up the equipment, catering and tables and chairs, often sending Zoe home early.

As the manager responsible for the challenging task of engaging and connecting with the community, Zoe was so appreciative of Chris's attitude. It made such a difference to have him so supportive, prepared to do all the heavy lifting.

The difference between Chris's service and Claire's self-centered attitude was night and day.

Chris, even though he was Zoe's subordinate, was demonstrating great leadership through his selfless service. As leaders we don't need a title to be effective in our service, just the willingness to put others' needs ahead of our own.

Service and Position

If we are a service-focused leader, we do not see our superior rank, authority within a family or position of power as a reason to stop serving. We see it in fact as a greater opportunity to serve a broader vision more effectively, and impact people and in a more profound way.

> *Life's most persistent and urgent question is:*
> *What are you doing for others?*
> —Martin Luther King Jr.

We don't see the job, family or group we are part of, or the people in it, as a vehicle to satisfy the agenda of our own life. We use our life as a vehicle to serve the people and cause(s) we are invested in.

We can, for instance, take the benefits of a salary and the stature of a position in a political party, but use that role purely for our gain or to satisfy our ambitions, without ever genuinely serving the organisation or people we are supposed to be representing.

Service and Giving

The manifestation and evidence of the heart attitude of service is found in the action of giving.

We can't serve without giving. To serve someone or something else means we have to give something of our-self. Service to others always comes at a cost, which can take the form of our time, goals, ego, energy, resources or even the ultimate example of selfless sacrifice, the cost of our own life.

On the twenty-fifth of April 1915, thousands of young Australians landed in foreign Gallipoli in World War I to fight for the freedom of their nation. After the campaign ended, more than eight thousand Australian soldiers had given their lives, but their wartime heroics had changed the destiny of their country.

Today, in homage to the Australians and New Zealanders who died in wars and peacekeeping operations, April 25, is referred to and commemorated in over twenty-one countries around the world.[55]

The ANZACS are honoured and esteemed not necessarily because of their high standing in society, their academic prowess, their talents or skills, but because of their demonstration of selfless service.

Everyone can be great, because everyone can serve.
—Martin Luther King Jr.

If we are a self-focused leader, we may be just taking people's effort, performance, skills, affection, time and energy and misguidedly using all of that to simply promote our own interests. This practice is usually exhausting for others, as we become a drain on the people connected to us if our relationship is only ever a one-way transaction that always favours us.

> *The selfish leader will attempt to lead others for their own gain and for the detriment of others.*
> —Tom Peters

The Power of Selfless Service

Selfless service and the act of giving opens up a pathway for individuals, groups and communities to move forward—often where they could not move past a boundary or reach a particular achievement themselves.

We sometimes hear an athlete or performer who wins an award tell the story of how a parent or family member sacrificed so much to provide them with an opportunity to attain their goal. When actress Regina King won her 2019 Academy Award, she tearfully thanked her mother in her acceptance speech, explaining 'I'm an example of what it looks like when support and love is poured into someone'.[56]

The politician who accepts victory in an election has likewise only achieved the result through the services and sacrifice of many volunteers who performed quite inglorious tasks, such as handing out how-to-vote cards at a polling booth or delivering flyers to letterboxes. Small acts of service can have significant consequences. Our giving may trigger a chain of positive events in the lives of others that carries on in a way we may never anticipate.

Great achievers often stand victorious on a platform of giving created by others.

After breaking world sprinting records and becoming the first American woman to win three gold medals in a single Olympiad at the 1960 Rome Olympics, Wilma Rudolph was crowned 'the fastest woman in the world'. However, were it not for the sacrificial service of her mother Blanche and some of her twenty-one siblings, she may never have walked again after age four. Born prematurely into extreme poverty, Wilma suffered numerous childhood diseases, including scarlet fever, pneumonia, whooping cough, measles, chickenpox and polio, which left her in leg braces and without the use of her left leg.

Told by doctors to prepare for a life as a disabled adult—that she would never walk again—Wilma did not suffer this fate, because her mother, Blanche, determined a different future for her daughter. For five years, on her one day off each week from her cleaning job, Blanche took her daughter the 160-kilometre round trip to and from the Nashville Hospital to undertake physical therapy. Mrs. Rudolph even learnt the recommended massage routine for her daughter's limbs from the specialists in Nashville, also teaching it to some of her older children to apply at home. At age twelve, as a result of the regular physical therapy and massage, Wilma stunned doctors by removing her leg braces and walking. Just four years later, at age sixteen, she travelled to Australia, where she would win a bronze medal in the 1956 Olympic Games, before going on to her unprecedented feat of winning three gold medals at the next Olympic Games, in 1960.

Such was her impact around the globe and the significance of her record-breaking career that Wilma was inducted into the US Olympic Hall of Fame.

She was selected as one of the Women's Sports Foundation's five greatest women athletes in the United States. The Wilma Rudolph Foundation was established to promote amateur athletics. The United States Postal Service issued a postage stamp in recognition of her accomplishments. And at least twenty-one books on Rudolph's life have been published. *Wilma: The Story of Wilma Rudolph*, her autobiography, was adapted into a television docudrama, and her life is also remembered in *Unlimited* (2015), a short documentary film for school audiences.[57]

Would this story be so if her mother had not had a heart of sacrificial service for her daughter, compelled by love to forfeit her one day of rest each week for an arduous travel schedule to attend treatment? If her brothers and sisters had decided to play outside rather than massaging her leg? In the same way, her siblings aren't even given names in this story, the actions of our service may not be highlighted or recognised. Yet, the impact may ultimately echo through eternity.

The Cycle of Giving and Receiving

When we start to serve and to give, we activate the cycle of giving and receiving. We can never reap if we never sow, and we can never receive if we never give. For example, we can't receive the rewards of seeing someone else's life grow if we never give from our own life to invest into them.

Giving, breaks the chains of our self-focus and also our anxiety of not having enough. If we're clutching things tightly to our chest, we're afraid of losing them, we're actually living in fear. This fear is of losing what we have and of not gaining more. If we are driven by a desire to accumulate more and achieve more purely for our self-indulgence, this creates a certain energy within us and a paradigm in our thinking that starts to dominate our decision-making.

When our hand is so tightly clenched around what we have to avoid losing it, the same hand is also unable to receive or take anything new that comes to it. If our hand is open, however, we can allow things to freely pass through, both to receive them and also to pass them on.

Giving opens the door to a different dimension than what we can typically access in the transactional fee-for-service model. Under the principles of the traditional 'buying and selling' structure, we pay for something based on its value, and we charge a price in exchange for the quality of service or product we provide. When we give, however, we operate outside this realm. We're motivated to act based on our care, not on our expectant reward. Understanding this concept is the doorway that leads us out of the limitations of mere transactions, and into the limitless cycle of sowing and reaping.

Only by giving are you able to receive more than you already have.
—Jim Rohn

The Challenge of Service

Service and giving can be challenging, even countercultural concepts for us to grapple with in today's society, rife with 'me-first' messages of self-promotion, self-fulfilment and self-development. To willingly serve another person, vision or cause is even confronting to our human nature, which can be deeply rooted in the behaviours of self-defence, self-awareness and self-survival.

It's one thing to put our shoulder to the wheel, work hard and endure pain when we can see a gain for ourself in the future. But when called to make all those sacrifices to advance the cause of someone or something else, it becomes a different proposition. Self-service comes naturally. Service to others, if involving self-denial, is more challenging.

James Gobbo is a remarkable example of rising above self, to serve the public. He moved from Italy to Australia at age seven. Though he spoke no English, he displayed aptitude in school, was in due course accepted into the University of Melbourne and in 1951 was awarded a Rhodes Scholarship to study at Oxford. He went on to work as a barrister in Melbourne, Australia, then was a judge of the Supreme Court of Victoria from 1978 to 1994. For his service, Sir James was honoured with knighthood in 1982. He was appointed Governor of Victoria in 1997, the first ever person of a non-English speaking background.[58]

> *The essentials of leadership are all about the use of one's talent in the interests of society.*
> —Sir James Gobbo

There are many 'justifiable' reasons why the philosophy of service does not or should not apply to us in specific situations. There are typically many self-focused needs in our life that call for us to prioritise them before meeting anyone else's—this is an inherent human trait, and one not easily overcome.

> *The first and best victory is to conquer yourself; to be conquered by yourself is of all things most shameful and vile.*
> —Plato

These self-serving demands take many forms, but ultimately all have the consistent theme of prioritising our own needs ahead of others'. I have termed them the '10 P's of Self'.

The 10 P's of Self

As a quick self-assessment exercise, you can rate yourself on a scale of 0 (very untrue) to 10 (very true) on the following statements. After contemplating your responses, you may notice some clear outliers that have crept unwittingly into your thinking and values. I did. Once I became aware of them, I was able to catch them if they recurred in my thinking and lifestyle, and with a concerted effort I adjusted them accordingly over time. But I also acknowledge that these questions are best reviewed often, as they act as a safeguard to my thinking and motivations at any given time.

- **Possessions:** I continually desire to have and own more things

- **Power:** In general, I want authority and control over people, decisions and resources

- **Pleasure:** I pursue and satisfy personal gratification as a daily priority in my life

- **Popularity:** I need to be liked and need to gain the approval and endorsement of others

- **Praise:** I desire positive affirmation from others to feel good about myself

- **Priorities:** I place personal interests ahead of others' concerns

- **Passiveness**: I am undisturbed by anyone else's situation or problems, as long as it doesn't affect me

- **Pride:** I believe that my achievements, knowledge, values or position are so important they put me above others, and I deserve to be served

- **Performance:** I need to win at all times and all costs and could not put anything ahead of staying number one

- **Perspective:** I'm unable to see my life outside the context of the immediate situation that makes me feel content or satisfied

Perspective allows us to see our life in the context of a bigger picture and broader plan. Without this perspective, we function from a strictly 'me-first' mentality, and our vision is narrowed down to focus primarily on ourselves and our immediate needs. We then tend to evaluate circumstances with two questions in mind that we use to guide our decision-making:

1. What will this cost me?

2. How will it benefit me?

Service and Assignment

When we are self-focused, we make decisions mainly through the perspective of this personal cost/benefit scoreboard, and this can restrict our ability to give and serve. If there is too high a personal cost or too little personal benefit, then it's unlikely we'll pursue these options.

However, when our life begins to connect with a sense of assignment that involves something bigger than us, our perspective shifts and our motivation moves toward achieving a mission more significant than just meeting our own needs.

Without this broader perspective or purpose calling us upward, 'we' become the assignment. We are mentally and emotionally consumed with self-gratification, trapped in an inward-looking lifestyle that is reflected in our decision-making.

When we connect with a broader purpose, rather than every situation being an opportunity to promote or satisfy our self-interests, our wants and needs start to take second priority to the achievement of this higher calling, and our self-focused goals, dreams and desires even become irrelevant when set beside the achievement of the higher purpose. For example, sweeping the floor of a community centre may be seen by one person as 'beneath' him or her. But to another person who carries a heartfelt belief that the centre will play a vital role in positively shaping the values and education of the community for future generations, it's an entirely different view. Sweeping the floor seems a natural act of contributing to bringing that vision to life.

We all still have personal needs. The *10 Ps of Self* listed above still clamour for our attention. But when we serve selflessly they cease to become the primary driving energy in our life. We have developed the ability to rise above the call to simply serve our own ambition and are able to choose to serve the needs of the higher calling.

The ability to choose to serve a cause bigger than just our own needs is the key to moving into higher levels of selfless service.

> *The sole meaning of life is to serve humanity.*
> —Leo Tolstoy

An Act Versus a Lifestyle

An act of service can be seen in the example of someone volunteering to take on the role of cooking the barbecue at a community fun day.

An act of service is admirable.

A lifestyle of service, however, moves into another dimension of serving, where there is no official start and end time, but rather, our entire life has become centred around the purpose of serving others and a higher calling. When we enter this level of service, we have taken up the assignment of serving another individual, a group, an organisation or a vision in a full-time capacity, and our life is now structured around that goal.

Only a life lived in service to others is worth living
—Albert Einstein

Service and Leadership

No vision can be fulfilled without anyone serving it. That's why service is an essential requirement if any idea, no matter how big or small, is to come to fruition. When we submit ourselves to serving—whether an assignment, a cause, a person or a community—we become leaders in that field. *The fastest way for us to become leaders of anything is to serve the people and purpose.*

Academic qualifications, titles and previous achievements do not make us leaders of anything. The guaranteed pathway to effective leadership is through the service of whatever we are connected to. The greater the measure of our surrender, selflessness and service, the greater the weight and impact of our leadership.

When our leadership does not have a strong focus on service, it has not developed to the point that it will impact anything or anyone in a significant manner.

Without service being a foundation of our leadership, we are prone to revert to self-focused leadership where we can, even subconsciously, skew our decision-making and goal-setting to suit our personal needs and agenda.

When we lead with selfless service as our primary motivation, it helps keep our intentions and actions honourable and well-directed.

Servant Leadership

Robert Greenleaf founded the Greenleaf Centre for Servant Leadership in 1964 after taking an early retirement from his corporate career, suspicious of the authoritarian leadership style prominent in US institutions. He became fascinated with the idea that the leader could also be the servant and published his first essay in 1970, now a book, *The Servant as Leader*, where he states: 'The servant–leader is servant first. That person is sharply different from one who is leader first. The only truly viable institutions will be those that are predominantly servant led'.[59]

The Asian Greenleaf Centre for Servant Leadership found, in further research, that where a work team had a servant leader, it was more likely to understand the goal and feel confident in its ability to perform well; that company performance, as measured by return on assets, was higher in companies led by CEOs who engaged in servant leadership; and that servant leaders gain team member trust and build long-term relationships by showing genuine concern for all members, which in turn elicits mutual cooperation—team members care about each other, and that enables them to be optimistic about their team's capabilities to be effective.[60]

Good leaders must first become good servants.
—Robert Greenleaf

As we adopt the value of selfless service into our leadership, we see our success as a leader measured by how well we are positively impacting others, not how great we can be in our own right.

Some people in leadership roles see themselves as positioned at the high point of a triangle. But as service leaders, we see the pyramid turned upside down, ourselves at the bottom point, providing a foundation and support for everyone around us.

Like Sidney Meyer, a Russian immigrant who arrived in Australia in 1899 as a penniless twenty-one-year-old not speaking English. He and his brother established a humble drapery business before growing it into the Myers Department Stores in 1920, and by 1926 he employed over 2,000 staff. He viewed these staff as family and community, caring for them deeply. He provided free vacations to managers and a sick fund for staff; shared holiday homes and even established a free hospital in the department store itself.

Staff frequently enjoyed social activities such as balls, picnics and sporting events. When the Great Depression was at its worst in 1931, Sidney Myer implemented a 20 per cent pay cut for all staff for eighteen months, immediately including himself in the wage reduction. He lowered wages, but only with the view to offering more people employment, and proactively encouraged other business leaders to do the same.

In the midst of everyone grabbing and taking what they could to survive, he bucked the trend and increased his giving and service to others.

He donated £22,000 (around $2M US in today's terms) of his personal wealth to the government to commence significant construction projects to enable more workers to be employed, and in 1930 hosted a Christmas dinner for 10,000 people with free transport and a present for every child who attended. His service and donations to other community projects were endless. Even after he died in 1934, his will mandated that 10 per cent of his wealth go to the charitable and educational needs 'of the community in which I made my fortune'.

A love for people, and a desire to serve them, characterised his leadership approach.[61]

I am not a politician; I do not seek publicity, nor have I any ulterior motive whatsoever, except my love for Australia and the Australian people.
—Sidney Myer

We've likely all been exposed to the enticing imagery and allure of being a leader 'at the top', holding a lot of power and having access to all the perks. But what we're talking about here is service and sacrifice, and there's rarely anything glamorous about that. It involves surrender, humility and the ability to lay down our self-interests and needs for the sake of progressing or benefitting someone else's situation or cause. In extreme cases, even laying down our lives.

When we lead with selfless service, we see our life as a seed that is to be sown into the ground to bear fruit for others.

Chapter Seven – Selfless Service

Two politicians, Hannah and Anthony, were elected to their respective seats in the constituency they represented.

Anthony's party had held the seat for over thirty years, being rarely troubled by even a slight dip in their approval rating or polling numbers. He entered politics through his father's connections and was established as a candidate more so as a family favourite than through a strategic party decision or vote amongst members. Anthony was looked on as a shining light by the party, a great media performer well versed in political spin to look and sound comfortable amidst the curliest of interviews. Having his eyes on a prominent portfolio position, he had been mentioned as taking a seat amongst the inner leadership of the party, and maybe even further.

Anthony saw little need to attend his local branch meetings and discuss issues with local members. Rarely—outside of election campaigns—was he seen amongst his community other than for photoshoots and media stunts. He hardly ever took time just to talk or listen to his constituents. He is a big fish in a reasonably small pond, promoting policies he knows are popular with the leadership, even if his local constituents oppose them, just to press his case for inclusion in the higher ranks of government. Anthony's position, and the people who voted for him, were nothing more than a means to achieve his self-serving goal, complete with subsequent salary and government perks. Anthony knew if he could just spend one term in office in the inner leadership, he would be financially set for life.

Hannah, likewise was elected to a comfortably safe seat, but Hannah had a deep-seated desire to serve the people. She attended almost every local branch meeting, often driving long distances, sometimes only to join an audience of five to six. She would sit and talk and listen, and then diligently relay the key messages and issues that mattered most to her constituents to the party. She didn't have the polish, grooming or turn of phrase Anthony had, and as such she had never really been considered for promotion.

Anthony and Hannah have the same role, but completely different motivations, and those on the ground knew which of them were fulfilling their leadership mandate.

If serving is below you, leadership is beyond you.
Unknown

Service Leadership Creates a Culture

While service may not be the most natural part of our human makeup, it can be taught and we can develop our capacity to serve. When we as leaders are willing to learn or be trained in the pattern of selfless service, we can begin to model it.

When we model a pattern of selfless service, we establish a standard within our family, business or community group.

This standard creates a culture of service, where everyone is more inclined to give than take, and this lays a foundation for success in any environment.

As much as we may like to think we can present an image to impress others to follow us, in the end, people will see through our motivations and agendas if we are not genuine. If we are self-focused or in the game for only *our* benefit, or we're asking more of others than we're giving, people will be less likely to commit to us or any broader vision we are promoting.

If not prepared to serve anything other than myself, how can I expect those connected to me to do any different?

The Lasting Impact of Service

While many leaders come and go throughout history, people who live a genuine life of giving and service are never forgotten. Their impact on those around them and their environment continues to echo throughout time.

The famous Roman Catholic nun Mother Teresa at just eighteen years of age left her family and all the familiarity of home in Macedonia, setting off to Ireland to become a nun.

A year later she took only three identical outfits, a pair of sandals and a tin washing pail to live and work among the poorest of the poor in remote India. After sowing the best years of her life into this vision, in 1979 at age sixty-nine, she was awarded the Nobel Peace Prize At the time of her death, in 1997, her charity operated 610 missions in 123 countries. These included hospices and homes for people with leprosy and tuberculosis, soup kitchens, children and family counselling programs, orphanages and schools. She had inspired over one million co-workers to join her vision. She is now Saint Teresa of Calcutta.[62]

Give your hands to serve and your hearts to love.
Mother Theresa

Leadership, through giving and the selfless service of others, always creates an impact.

CHAPTER EIGHT

Pioneering Spirit

Pioneer: a person who is among those who first enter or settle a region, thus opening it for occupation and development by others

Spirit: the inner character of a person, thought of as different from the material person we can see and touch

When we carry a pioneering spirit, we break new ground. We demonstrate an ability to forge new paths, break through existing boundaries and enter territories that were previously off-limits. We set new standards, re-establish accepted norms and create an opportunity for others to move into these areas with us and dwell in a new landscape.

When we're operating with a pioneering spirit, we're not content to fit quietly within the current scene. We exert outwardly the inner energy that pushes toward a preferred future we believe will bring positive change, now and to future generations. We carry a vitality inside us that urges us to enter new frontiers and establish new opportunities.

We are not caught by the wave of conventionalism, not anchored by the weight of tradition, but have broken free of environmental constraints to surge forward to chart the future we dream of.

Like the explorer hacking a way through the thick overgrowth of the jungle, as pioneer leaders, we are likely to encounter major obstacles. Pioneering is a grueling, gut-wrenching task and typically calls for our blood, sweat and tears in the ultimate test of our resolve to push through against the odds.

The way of the pioneer is always rough.
—Harvey Firestone

We are often seen in a negative light by the current establishment for disturbing the standards and norms in the status quo. Our forward progress displaces the settled landscape and is in itself a confrontation to the accepted trends.

Our efforts as a pioneer sometimes need to be seen through the lens of history to see the positive impact we bring to our sphere of influence.

Rebels and non-conformists are often the pioneers and designers of change.
—Indira Gandhi

Socrates was tried for impiety and for corruption of the youth of Athens in 399 BC on the basis that he failed to recognise the set of Athenian gods the city acknowledged. An unconventional thinker and nonconformist, , he consistently challenged the status quo of the government and society by posing uncomfortable and unsettling questions. In views that clashed with Athenian authorities and its citizens, he insisted the greater importance was on the development of the mind rather than on clinging to past glories, notions of wealth and a fixation on physical beauty. He even told his jurors they were concerned with their families, careers and political responsibilities instead of the 'welfare of their souls'. Found guilty at one of the most famous trials in history, he was sentenced to death through the drinking of a poisonous hemlock concoction. But today history credits Socrates as the founder of Western philosophy, his methods of questioning still used in classrooms and law-school debate to get to the bottom of underlying issues of the matter. You will also find numerous busts of him in academic institutions in recognition of his contribution to education.[63]

Defining a True Pioneer

The characteristic of the pioneer in the context of this book refers to those who see a brighter future that does not harm others or involve an involuntary surrender of others' rights or their will. They are not intent on undermining positive, healthy aspects of a well-functioning society, and are not dangerous 'fanatics', as described by psychologist Steve Eichel, President of the International Cultic Studies Association, a group with a mission 'to study psychological manipulation, especially as it manifests in cultic and related groups'.[64]

He describes the propaganda and mindset of cult leaders and fanatics as 'sounding strikingly like hygienists who seek to clean or sanitise an environment in order to make it a healthier place to live. Fanatics utilise 'us vs, them' language and divide the world in a polarized manner between that-which-promotes-health vs. that-which-causes-illness'.[65]

This then leads to the obvious logic behind their actions to eradicate the diseased people and establish a society totally compliant with their worldview.

While the characteristics of pioneer leaders we are describing here do carry a conviction and a burning desire to bring reformation, it is never at the expense of human harm or the freedom of choice of the individual.

A Picture of the Pioneer Leader

As pioneer leaders, we are not molded into the shape of the prevailing culture. Instead, we are formed by the internal conviction that drives us, fashioned by the set of values that defines us and led by a vision that compels us. Developed to the point where it is now stronger than the external culture, our internal culture is the primary reference point to guide us and the fuel source to carry us.

As pioneer leaders, in our efforts to bring positive transformation, we create an impact on the environment similar to the pack-breaking marathon runner. The runners typically form into a pack, settling into an informally agreed-upon, comfortable tempo. However, when a breakaway runner accelerates and leaves the group, it upsets the rhythm of the pack; runners are forced to decide to join the breakaway runner or stay behind in the mob. Our pioneering leadership has a similar effect, as we break ranks to run at our own pace and rhythm, different from those around us. Our intent is not to simply create disturbance or aggravation for the sake of it, but our efforts to see something new established can often create disruption to the status quo.

The Price of the Pioneer

When we move into the realm of pioneer leadership, we don't follow the footsteps of the majority or necessarily comply with the politically correct, who either consciously or unconsciously subject themselves to the prevailing cultural norms. Such can be the conforming gravitational force exerted by the concept of 'normal' that even if these standards are destructive, even if not agreeing with them, the majority may uphold them. Pioneering is not a comfortable journey. As pioneer leaders we have to accept that in the pursuit to establish something new, we may often be alone, criticised, attacked and ridiculed.

Galina Starovoytova entered Russian politics in 1989. She led a fierce fight for democracy, minority-group justice and a reduction of the power of the secret police, the KGB. She was a key advisor to President Boris Yeltsin.

Starovoytova reportedly compiled a dossier implicating the Communist Party in corruption. Supporters claimed she planned to present her evidence in the lower house of parliament, of which she was a deputy, in the coming week.

But she was brutally gunned down before she had the chance. In June 2005, the two assassins, who included former GRU Main Intelligence Directorate, Yuri Kolchin, were brought to trial and convicted of murder. The GRU reports to the military, not the president. President Boris Yeltsin stated that 'The shots that cut short the life of Galina Starovoytova wounded every Russian who cherished democratic values'. More than ten thousand Russian citizens paid their respects when her body lay in state.[66]

Pioneers may be picturesque figures,
but they are often rather lonely ones.
—Nancy Astor

Leadership Upgrade

The Impact of Pioneers on the Status Quo

In every environment, whether it's a home, family, political party, community or business, there is a prevailing and existing status quo called a *culture*. Culture is best described as 'the way we do things around here', and it manifests through routines, rituals, rules, symbols, stories, systems, values and beliefs. The culture in the environment exerts pressure on anyone within it to conform. This pressure can be visible in written rules and verbal directions, or it can be invisible, subtle and unspoken. But it is present, and it is an active force working upon everyone under it.[67]

When we carry a set of values and standards that are inconsistent with the prevailing culture, it is effectively a 'counterculture'.

This clash of cultures creates a tension when the two cultures interact. The conflict created between the two different belief systems, ideologies, philosophies and values will tend to escalate. As the pioneering, challenging party in the battle, we may be subject to attacks, threats or intimidation from the established cultural gatekeepers, calling us to compromise and align with their views.

Martin Luther changed the Christian Church forever in the sixteenth century by publicly confronting some of the foundational beliefs of Roman Catholicism and sparked the Protestant Reformation.

A theological scholar, Luther became disillusioned by what he believed were inaccurate interpretations of scripture and corruption, where he witnessed Catholic Church clergy promoting good works such as financial donations, instead of faith, to secure salvation. He wrote of his concerns in his famous '95 Theses' pamphlet, a devastating critique of the conventions of the church, and proceeded to nail it to the University of Wittenberg's chapel door. The document quickly spread throughout Europe, posing a serious destabilizing

Chapter Eight – Pioneering Spirit

force for the Catholic Church.

In response, he was ordered to retract his objections, but refused unless the Church could prove him wrong by use of the scriptures. The pope then formally wrote to Luther, demanding he retract his statements or face excommunication. A letter Luther duly burnt! He was immediately excommunicated.

He then faced further persecution when, in 1521, he was summoned before a general assembly of secular authorities known as the Diet of Worms—and there declared a 'convicted heretic', a condemned and wanted man. While hiding in seclusion under the threat of arrest in 1522, he formed the Lutheran Church, which ultimately spread across Europe and around the world. His teachings radically changed Christian theology forever.

Luther's pioneering leadership has positioned him as one of the most influential figures in Western civilisation during the last millennium.[68]

If we are moving into the dimension of pioneering leadership, it may become effectively untenable to stay in our current role, network or structure. It may mean we branch out to follow our own vision in the interests of being faithful to our calling, and we begin the process of building a community around that culture, first small and then larger.

Alternatively, it may be possible to influence the existing structure, birthing a new culture where our inspired and transforming leadership changes the existing environment's values and norms.

In 2014, Piyush Gupta, the CEO of DBS Bank of Singapore, challenged their dated approach to customer service, reinventing it as an industry-leading digital online service. Initially, however, he faced an entrenched culture that was slow-moving and relied on fifty-year-old-software. He told his staff, 'banks are yesterday's story', Gupta explained. And that they were 'competing against start-up companies with a drive and energy that large incumbent companies like ours just don't have. If we don't change our current approach, we will not survive'. DBS was named the 'World's Best Digital Bank' by Euromoney in 2016 and increased net profits by 36 per cent. In 2019, Gupta was the first ever Singapore CEO to be included in the world's Top 100 CEOs by the Harvard Business Review.[69]

As pioneer leaders, we are less concerned by issues such as job security, our reputation or peer approval. We are more concerned with integrity of approach, introduction of positive change and fulfilment of the vision in our heart.

Characteristics of a Pioneering Leader

We will know we are entering into the dimension of a pioneer leader when we start to exhibit several of the following key traits:

i. **We live in two time zones simultaneously.**

    While we live in the *today* of now, we also have the ability to live in the *tomorrow* of the future. This future is what we are longing to make a reality.

    Motivational speaker and leadership coach Marcus Buckingham explains that 'leaders are fascinated by the future. The friction between what is and what can be burns you, stirs you up and propels you. This is leadership'.[70]

    As pioneer leaders we see the future so clearly in our mind and can visit it so vividly it's almost as if we are in two places at one point in time. When we come to this point, we have the capacity to consistently and mentally access our preferred reality and landscape, and possibly figuratively live in that dimension more so than the current one. Our vision of the future is real enough to us that it can be clearly described and communicated to others to allow them to access it also.

ii. **The inspiration of the call provides our internal fuel**

We have an ability to remain *up* and *positive* internally, by energising ourselves with the inspiration of our vision. We are not reliant on external motivators, and this ability helps maintain the health of our self-life so we can keep our mood and emotions positive and our thinking patterns optimistic. It guards against the onset of cycles of negative thinking that revolve around fears and limitations that if dwelt upon, begins a harmful internal dialogue that paves a pathway to our own defeat.

Maya commenced her role as the CEO of an online counselling service funded by service organisations and business donations. After being established by the founding members in response to a string of suicides that affected their family, the counselling service had been operating for sixteen years with a loyal band of followers.

Maya, a high performer, was passionate about its potential to save lives and inspired by the call to provide support to people suffering who had nowhere else to go. A no nonsense person, she was committed to achieving results.

Within twenty minutes of her first day on the job, it was apparent to her the existing culture needed serious reform; for months on end staff left basic tasks uncompleted; decisions from meetings went unimplemented; there were no processes to carry out basic functions, no measures to monitor performance or outcomes; staff and volunteers worked on whatever activities and tasks they liked, rather than what the organisation needed, and piles of paperwork from five years ago littered the desk.

The next day Maya arrived at work in overalls. An industrial-sized waste-disposal bin had been delivered at the kerbside. Calling all the staff and volunteers together, she declared, 'Get your gloves on. Today—we clean!' Yesterday's baggage was being removed. And any redundant paperwork, equipment or grime, being evicted. A new day, a new era.

Over the next three months Maya shared her vision with volunteers and staff. She reoriented their priorities on tasks that would create success, inviting everyone to stay and make a contribution, but she also made it clear what the direction, focus and expectations were of everyone, and that they would be accountable to deliver on the key performance indicators she established.

However, at the end of three months, all but one of the existing staff had left or been let go, half of the board had departed and even volunteers decided the changing environment was too uncomfortable to stay when 'compared to how good things used to be'.

When asked by the board if she was concerned about all the people leaving, Maya remarked, 'Oh no, I'm much more excited by the people who are staying, and the new ones that are coming'.

Despite the turnover, performance had actually lifted remarkably. Staff and volunteers who previously bemoaned the slapdash approach were rejuvenated and reveled in being part of something with an organised edge to it. More calls were being fielded, more referrals to specialised support groups and crisis clinics , and more positive feedback.

The new momentum created additional funding. Donors came forward. New volunteers and positive media about the organisation had never been so prevalent. The place was buzzing. Within twelve months, Maya's pioneering leadership transformed the atmosphere, standards and performance, pushing through the existing culture and resetting long-held standards and behaviours.

As a pioneer leader, the inspiration we receive from revisiting our vision and our calling creates forward momentum within us, establishing a strong sense of hope, and focuses our thinking on what's possible.

iii. We open a pathway for others

Pioneers establish a pathway that others can travel on to access the same place we have journeyed to. There, others can enjoy the benefits of the new environment we have established, join our work and continue to grow it, even if we are the ones who pay the price to establish it.

> *Pioneers get slaughtered, and the settlers prosper.*
> —Daymond John

While others can reap the benefits of the new territory we opened as a pioneer, the actual work of the pioneer leader is unique, like tools crafted to perform a specific task that other tools cannot.

Therefore, our role as a pioneer is crucial, because if we don't open up an access path for others to walk into, they may never experience it. If we don't pioneer a new standard, pattern or norm, there may be no one else with the capacity to do so, leaving many trapped in the existing protocols of the current environment.

iv. **We reset standards**

What is considered '*normal*' in our family, community, faith group, workplace team, etc., exists because those patterns and values have been established, endorsed and promoted by leaders, either past or present, who held a place of authority, validating or invalidating the status quo.

As pioneer leaders, we have the ability to reset *normal* to a different standard. We carry a weight and stature that authorises an upgraded version of what's acceptable, and we supersede previous leadership endorsements. We lay out a new benchmark that simultaneously cancels the old as obsolete and sets a new standard that others can live under, adopt and promote within their own lives, families and communities.

New Zealander Grant Douglas was just five years old when his father led him into the garage to watch him commit suicide with a shotgun. He cites this horrific incident as the reason why at age thirteen, he turned to drugs, remaining addicted for the next thirty-six years—along the way leading his wife and six children into a life of drug addiction. 'I thought the only way I could get my kids to love me was to supply them with drugs', Grant reflected.

Domestic violence and financial mismanagement added

to the family dysfunctionality. At rock bottom, Grant connected with a men's support program, where he began to rebuild his life foundations, transitioning out of his addiction. He acknowledged that 'I had ruined my kids' life' and was determined to take responsibility to try and reverse the course he had started his family on. He set about mending broken relationships while supporting his wife and children to kick their own addiction. Now in his fifties, Grant can look back on his pioneering leadership that he applied to his own life, then helped his wife and children become drug free, reunited them as a functional family and established a new standard for their descendants.[71]

v. **We see a brighter future**

Our vision is a positive one, consisting of abundance, restoration, success and recovery—enlarged by faith and optimism, not limited by fear and intimidation.

The strength and attractiveness of this future we can see provides hope and inspiration to others, who connect with the excitement of entering this radically different future. It fuels a momentum in us and is transferred to those connected to us, empowering them to move past fears and limitations with boldness.

vi. **We accommodate others to join us**

As pioneer leaders, we create opportunities for others to join in the ownership and achievement of the vision we are moving towards and to contribute to the journey. It is not an exclusive club for a select few that seeks to keep others out unless they have a blatantly negative agenda to disrupt rather than contribute to the goals of the group.

We are able to provide opportunities for everyone to contribute their unique gifts and talents to advance the promise of a better future.

Barriers to Developing Pioneering Leadership

While the idea of being a pioneering leader sounds like a prestigious title and an exciting adventure, the reality is that there are typically several negating forces that can limit our access to this dimension of leadership.

i. Conformity

It's hard to change a culture when that culture is inside us. As long as our internal operating system remains shaped to conform to the patterns of behaviour and values of our environment, it's doubtful we will see a need to change it.

> *Everyone thinks of changing the world,*
> *but no one thinks of changing himself.*
> —Leo Tolstoy

If we are completely immersed in, accepting of and dependent on the systems and routines of the status quo, our internal culture is already primarily aligned with the outer norms, and we will lack the inner dynamics to pioneer a move to bring change.

As leaders with a pioneering spirit, we are not so conformed by the existing culture that we let ourselves be too attached to

Chapter Eight – Pioneering Spirit

it; otherwise, we limit our ability to be part of the solution, as we are already part of the problem.

ii. **Adverse Reaction**

Often, our introduction, or proposed introduction, of change brings a reaction against us. Even if in the best interests of many, if the change is going to have a negative impact on individuals, groups or networks, they are likely to react adversely.

Like the example of the marathon runners, the majority is challenged by being disturbed from their rhythm. They can attack the person or message that is creating a disturbance. If you kick the hornet's nest, you can expect to be confronted by angry hornets. The threat and the intimidation we feel as a result can potentially stop us from continuing or alter the direction of our pioneering work. The idea of creating tension with the establishment and those close to us can be overwhelming. To avoid the conflict, we may choose to compromise our calling or conviction.

When we function as a pioneering leader, though, we are prepared to accept that no matter how much we try to diffuse or avoid it, conflict is a necessary part of our journey into new territory. We are not seeking to create conflict. But we are not willing to compromise our message or conviction to prevent it.

iii. **Comfort and Convenience**

Doing nothing is easier than doing something. Usually, our natural inclination is, in general, to maximise the level of comfort experienced in our daily life by staying within the existing norms of our community and culture.

However, continually prioritising what is comfortable and what is convenient can eventually create a mould around our life that we cannot break free from. As pioneering leaders, we are fundamentally opposed to choosing comfort and convenience over the pursuit of our dream and vision. We push away the temptation and patterns of a lifestyle that simply serves our own immediate physical, emotional or mental needs , so these things do not limit the pursuit of our dream.

iv. Consistency

Pushing against the resistance of long-standing boundaries in the environment can be exhausting, and being the target of the gatekeepers of prevailing culture can be demoralising and hurtful.

Consistency is an essential part of our pioneering journey because as long as we actively pursue our dream, we have a chance to succeed. No one who ever gave up has ever won.

But if we do not see progress in our pursuits, it becomes harder to stay in the race. We have potential at this point to become inconsistent in our approach, wondering if it's all worth it, or if we will ever break through.

Pioneers are the ones who get arrows in their backs.
—Brian Roberts

Our mind, body, soul and spirit as a pioneer can take a pounding during our journey, so we need to know we are vulnerable to these impacts. That's why we must keep ourselves continually energised by the vision of our mission, aligned to the direction we committed to and connected to close friends and leaders who support and cover us. This practice will help ensure we remain consistent, that we stay engaged in our race and that we build endurance and longevity to endure our journey until our goals come to fruition.

v. Lack of Connections

If we are not connected to the right people, who can cover and support us against the barbs and attacks of the opposition, and the sheer workload of the task we are called to, it's challenging to maintain a pioneering leadership calling. These connections can also call forth our potential to pursue a pioneering leadership path when things get tough.

Being isolated and without support when we're facing opposition over an extended period is a recipe for defeat, even for the strongest and most determined.

We must be connected to people who can protect and provide for us emotionally, mentally and relationally.

The Call to Advancement

As pioneer leaders, we carry an energy and momentum within us to build, advance, develop and grow. We are not interested in merely existing, maintaining or simply surviving.

We understand the achievement of our vision is progressive, so there is always another step forward to take and another chapter of the story to write.

That's why the energy of our pioneering leadership is always to advance and progress. It is like a fresh, fast-flowing river surging and rushing through its riverbed in the countryside. In the face of this powerful flow there is little opportunity for anything to stand still or travel in a different direction. This picture depicts the momentum we create in our group, our environment and ourselves. It differs sharply from the view of a stagnant, stale, still body of water, often associated with the build-up of pond sludge, unpleasant odour and the presence of bacteria and disease, allowed to fester from a lack of activity and movement.

One can choose to go back toward safety
or forward toward growth.
Growth must be chosen again and again;
fear must be overcome again and again.
—Abraham Maslow

A Growth Mentality

Without a clear mandate to 'grow and go', our leadership, and those connected with us can settle into a rut. A pattern of maintenance and routine emerges that soon begin to resemble the picture of that stagnant body of water.

In the natural environment, dormant, inactive objects or locations are targets for infestation by insects and disease; they are subject to being overtaken by surrounding vegetation. The same is true with a mindset that has no growth or active energy to move and advance it.

In the corporate world, British Home Stores and Woolworths in the UK, Radio Shack and C&J Energy Services in the US, Japan's Skymark Airlines and Brazil's fourth-largest telecom operator, Oi, are examples of large, established companies that recently filed for bankruptcy, all largely due to their failure to continue to grow, develop and improve.[72]

That's why as soon as we feel an element of staleness or dormancy entering ourselves or those connected to us, we will quickly do something to freshen up the approach and provide a revised dynamic to keep the environment new and alive.

The Need for Continued Growth

The mantle of leadership in itself creates and demands growth in us as we become exposed to new responsibilities, new pressures, new challenges and new opportunities.

If we can't adapt, we will become redundant. An ability to respond accurately and increase our capacity to meet the requirements of the role enables us to continue to be effective. To function as a pioneering leader, we must keep shattering our internal borders of comfort and tradition.

Frances Hesselbein was appointed CEO of the Girl Scouts of the USA in 1976, at a particularly challenging time in its sixty-four-year history. Despite being the largest organisation for girls and women in the world, it had a declining membership, and its governance structure separated, rather than united, its individual branches. In fact, it was on the verge of falling into irrelevance. Society had changed significantly throughout the 1960s and '70s, and stay-at-home mothers were no longer the norm. Yet the Scouts still relied on drawing its members and volunteers from predominantly white middle-class families, who were focused on pursuing badges that related to housewife duties.

While not discarding these foundations, Hesselbein set about making the organisation less hierarchical and more relational and rebranded the marketing to appeal to more diverse community groups, tripling racial and ethnic minority membership. She also expanded the array of badges to include leadership, science and technology. A troop project these days may involve assisting a Mexican village gain access to pastuerised milk, a far more dynamic adventure than the woven potholders of a bygone Girl Scout era. In 1998, Hesselbein was awarded the Presidential Medal of Freedom for her work with the Girl Scouts of the USA.[73]

Success is on the other side of your comfort zone.
—Orrin Woodward

Even leaders who previously pioneered great things are at risk of becoming dormant and irrelevant if they choose to rest only in past efforts and past accomplishments.

The Hazard of Stagnant Leadership
The speed of the boss is the speed of the team.
—Lee Iacocca

If our leadership fails to provide *fresh food* (fresh thoughts, ideas, energy, challenges and innovations) to those connected to us so they can consume them and grow, after some time, several negative consequences have the potential to manifest:

1. Those connected to us will almost certainly be negatively affected by the dormant, decaying attitude we are carrying in our leadership. This attitude would manifest in their settling into familiar routines, relying on tradition rather than seeking innovation or productivity, and superficial efforts rather than passionately pursuing breakthrough. The

cutting-edge dynamic that created any success and momentum in the past would begin to fade. In short, they conform to the lukewarm, half-hearted approach we are expressing as the standard setter.

2. Group members may leave to seek a more growth-dynamic environment where there is some action. They may feel the atmosphere we are creating as a leader is not providing suitable opportunities for them to develop, grow, learn, impact the environment or achieve anything significant.

3. Group members may attempt to take over the leadership if they feel we have actually become a stumbling block and lack the leadership edge to reach our intended destination. This situation can even result in a leadership coup, a hostile takeover.

Areas of Growth to Focus on

When we function with a pioneering sharpness, we sustain our cutting edge as a leader and consequently keep our approach fresh. We also keep the atmosphere charged and the environment clean, where others are inspired and encouraged to move forward.

We develop these key areas:

i. **Personal growth**

We never stop learning, growing and developing, and we can never think we know it all. While we may have a sound base of understanding and experience, we also realise that for every topic, there is always another dimension of knowledge, skill and understanding we can move to.

> *Unless you try to do something beyond what you have already mastered, you will never grow.*
> —Ronald E. Osborne

We always need a plan to grow in every aspect of our lives, including relationships, finances, information, influence and achievements. This mentality sets a healthy dynamic and atmosphere that extends to our business, family or organisation. It creates a momentum in the environment that discourages those connected to us from settling for what is comfortable or familiar to them. It also establishes a culture that others can catch and informs new people entering in as to what 'normal' is.

ii. Growing in depth of understanding

We don't just settle for understanding the basics, but we press on to become experts—always seeking to build our understanding.

Driver Juan Manuel Fangio, nicknamed The Master, dominated the first decade of Formula One racing with four different teams, a feat never repeated. He dedicated himself to studying motor racing as a science and an artform in a never-ending pursuit to improve his skills, understanding and performance.

In the 1950 Monaco Grand Prix, flying out of a sharp, double bend chicane and approaching a blind turn with nothing in his field of vision ahead of him, he inextricably stomped on the brake. It was a move that saved his life and simultaneously won him the race. Just around the bend, hidden from sight of all approaching cars, was a multi-car pileup, which he avoided by slowing down.

Chapter Eight – Pioneering Spirit

His peers and commentators considered the braking a miracle. Why did he do it? Such was his commitment to master his craft, he had studied photographs of previous races at that track and in that location in 1936, fourteen years earlier, a similar accident had occurred. 'When I approached the turn, I noticed something different about the crowd, a different colour. I was leading but instead of seeing their faces looking at me, I was seeing the back of their heads. Something else had attracted their attention. I remembered the photograph and braked as hard as I could'.[74]

Sometimes when we achieve adequate competence, we can tend to settle into a familiar coping pattern of merely going through the motions. We can settle in the belief that we have already 'made it', which shuts down further creativity and inspiration. It can then effectively become a prison, holding us at our current capacity and level of growth.

A fisherman skilled at using a rod, if unable to let go of the old to explore further options, can forfeit the opportunity to learn to use a fishing net to increase productivity. What we have that is good can actually stop us from moving towards what is great.

When we are pioneering leaders, we carry a strong forward-oriented energy that keeps pushing against the limits of our current state and capacity, and it puts a healthy demand on us to grow.

iii. Growing in breadth of understanding

We don't need to know everything about everything, but it is beneficial to know something about most things, even what isn't our specialty.

We shouldn't limit ourselves by declaring, for instance, 'I'm not a numbers person', and decide to close off from developing any understanding of finances—where the money is going or how the books work. We need to continue to learn, even if in just a basic level of awareness, across a range of areas. Otherwise, we are in danger of:

1. having what we don't know be used against us if someone manipulates the information they are providing to steer us in a particular direction

2. or simply not seeing the reality of a situation clearly, completely unaware of the problems and danger in our environment that could potentially hurt us and those connected to us

Business consultant Sidney Yoshida pioneered the breakthrough concept of 'the iceberg of ignorance' in 1989, when his study found that 100 per cent of frontline problems were known to the frontline employees, but only 74 per cent to team leaders, 9 per cent to middle management and just 4 per cent to top management. This scenario could easily apply to a family, business or community environment. It serves as a powerful reminder about the need to stay connected to the people and information that give us an understanding of what's actually going on.[75]

It's what we can't see, or don't understand that has more potential to create damage than what we do know. We need to take responsibility to gain a general level of understanding and oversight about the approach being taken.

iv. Growing in capacity

By definition, the term 'capacity' *defines 'the maximum amount something can contain or produce'*.[76]

When the capacity of a power station drops, the people being supplied power are at risk of lights out and equipment failure. When our capacity as a leader grows, we are better able to consistently produce quality outcomes ourselves, and also supply those connected to us.

Some of us can simultaneously manage a business, work a full-time job, lead a community group and support a family of five successfully. In contrast, someone else may find just getting out of bed at 10 a.m. a challenge. It doesn't matter where we start. We all have a beginning point and a level we can grow from.

Developing capacity is as much about internal maturity as it is about actual skill levels. It's about our ability to 'carry' and 'produce', which is something we can develop over time.

But we limit our capacity if we do not learn to overcome any inhibiting mentalities, fears or disbelief in what is possible and what we can achieve. Some of us have never learnt to operate outside our natural comfort zone or the boundaries of our thinking. For example, we may never engage in physical exercise because we feel 'tired', but this may merely highlight our inability to move past our mental limitations and our undisciplined habits in this area. We remain trapped by the confines of what we feel is comfortable to us.

What separates us as a pioneering leader is our ability to grow in every aspect of life to accommodate the demands of our assignment, even if it is hard or uncomfortable. We develop a cyclical pattern of breaking personal limitations so we can grow into a greater stature, care more deeply for others, live with more passion and become more effective at moving toward our dreams.

v. Growing in influence and impact

As pioneering leaders, we are always seeking to expand our influence.

> *Before you are a leader success is all about growing yourself. When you become a leader, success is all about growing others.*
> —Jack Welch

Not only do we want to influence people connected to us, but also we look to increase our influence on those who oppose us, those who are undecided about us, those who are undecided what 'team' they are on, those above us, those below us, and the wider public in general. We speak at every opportunity to exercise our influence.

Growing in influence is a core outcome at the heart of our pioneering leadership. The alternative to influencing is to *be influenced*. But our make-up as a pioneering leader calls us to affect, not just be affected by, the environment around us.

vi. Growing in numbers

If having ten people strongly committed to our vision is good, then having twenty of the same mould is better. While we value those we have touched, we do not forget the others we

Chapter Eight – Pioneering Spirit

can potentially reach. We remain focused on the ones still out there, as much as those already with us. We do not settle for 'preaching to the converted' but have a burning desire to reach more people and bring them along.

A critical method of achieving this growth in numbers is to equip and activate those already connected to us to recruit and assimilate others.

vii. Growing in strength

If we are still lifting the same amount of weight after going to the gym regularly for five years, something's wrong.

We need to develop strength to move past obstacles and barriers, take on a project and get the job done, take a hit and keep moving forward, stand our ground without flinching, and become comfortable with the fact that not everyone is going to like us. Otherwise, we will lack the fortitude to make a dent in the environment, and we'll quickly become shut down and silenced. Without strength to push it into reality, our nice idea will stay just that, and remain on the inside of us forever.

In the jungle, there are many noises—made by the voices of a wide variety of creatures: animals, birds and insects. They fill the air with chatter, squawks, opinions and gossip that all contribute to a backdrop of background noise. But when the lion's roar booms across the landscape, everything in the vicinity falls silent in recognition of the strength of that voice's authority.

viii. Growing in vision

As we see our vision become a reality, we don't want to stop with what we've achieved. Instead, we're focused on the next step, the next phase of development. The vision of our assignment does not decrease, but grows and increases as we can see even more possibilities, new horizons and fresh opportunities to move toward.

Doug was desperate to escape his full-time job in the big bureaucracy, having decided it was time to urgently move into his own consultancy business. For months he worked furiously, toiling away to create the infrastructure he needed. He designed his website, created a logo, established his pricing, designed a letterhead and registered a business name. Excited that he had the foundation, he was ready to launch. But a casual question from a friend ('So, how are you going to get clients?') suddenly brought home the pointed realisation his vision had only extended to opening the doors. Quickly, he developed a fresh plan that involved a three-month marketing campaign. This did delay his launch, but proved an invaluable phase of filling his work funnel with jobs that ensured him start-up work and a successful transition.

If our progress is continual, then our vision needs to be as well, or we will end up arriving at our immediate destination and have nowhere else to go.

ix. Growing in character

While we can be glad to see growth in our profits, performance, influence, results or possessions, one of the crucial areas we must see growth in is character.

To have personal weaknesses, shortcomings or limitations is to be expected. However, these become an issue if the same deficiencies and immaturity are still having a repeatedly negative impact on us and those connected to us in five, ten or twenty years.

For example, we may have an inability to work through conflict constructively; where typically for us, such situations end negatively—we sever the relationship. If this is a recurring pattern over two decades, it demonstrates we lack adequate maturity within our character in this area. We are stuck in a negative pattern. By extension, it's unlikely those looking to us for leadership will be quick to forgive mistakes either or to maintain long-lasting relationships.

In this example, a growth in character would be demonstrated in our ability to be the bigger person, reach out to others and mend bridges, work through the issues constructively, love unconditionally and forgive, all the while maintaining the relationship. We can still draw appropriate boundaries where needed and acknowledge the implications of people's actions; we just don't allow ourselves to be bogged down keeping score of wrongdoings or past issues. We become big-hearted people—soft towards others—so we can let go of offence and remain free in our heart to keep moving toward our vision.

CHAPTER NINE

Breakthrough Thinking

Breakthrough: an act or instance of removing or surpassing an obstruction or restriction; the overcoming of a stalemate

Think: Have a particular mental attitude or approach

The quality of our thinking can decide the quality of our life, and therefore our leadership.

The voice of our mind can be our sharpest critic and create our biggest obstacles. Or it can be our greatest supporter, our most potent weapon to move past boundaries and into new frontiers. Our thoughts are unspoken words that carry the same energy and impact as spoken words, if not more. Thoughts become beliefs that manifest in our behaviours.

If we change our thinking, we change our life.

Breakthrough thinking is not about our level of intellect or academic prowess, but rather, our capacity to receive, capture and promote the thoughts that will elevate us beyond internal limitations and external opposition.

Breakthrough thinking is critical to our leadership success. It enables us to grow beyond mental constraints. When we connect with the right input, we can rise above these handicaps imposed on us by our mind that, by default, are otherwise at work within us. We can start to reconstruct our identity, reimagine possibilities and realign our sense of purpose. With inaccurate perceptions overthrown, our renewed mindset creates an internal transformation, bringing an empowering momentum that drives us forward.

The Impact of Thinking in Our Life

If we think well, we live well.

> *It all begins and ends in your mind. What you give power to has power over you.*
> —Leon Brown

Thoughts of success, victory, destiny, and purpose create an internal energy and momentum that open the wells of belief and boldness inside us. Negative thought patterns, by contrast, contaminate us from the inside, shutting down our vision, becoming the insidious 'enemy within' we can never defeat.

The Director of the Penn Positive Psychology Center, Martin Seligman, often described as 'the father of positive thinking', notes that positive thinking, and thinking like an optimist, is a crucial key to a leader coping with ups and downs, and bouncing back from setbacks.[77]

Negative Thinking

Negative forces that are at work in our mind are generally unconscious and undetected, but become repetitive, and have a very real effect on us.

Chapter Nine – Breakthrough Thinking

For many, negative thinking is a habit,
which over time, becomes an addiction.
—Peter McWilliams

Negative thoughts are planted in our mind like seeds, that take root and grow. They originate from the following sources:

i. **Negative past experiences**

For example, the pain from a failed relationship or a previous unsuccessful attempt to achieve something can become embedded and if unresolved can fester and infect our innermost being. Our mind then draws thoughts and energy from this pain every day, contaminating our thinking patterns for the rest of our life.

ii. **Words spoken by authority figures**

Negative words to or about us are particularly powerful when they come from authority figures.

Words, true or untrue, carry an energy and a power. If we are not equipped to refute the inaccurate, negative or damaging words spoken to us when we are young, they can result in a lifetime of debilitating thoughts.

Even for a mature adult, the judgmental or inaccurate words of a respected leader or father figure can have an equally long-lasting impact if we allow them to.

iii. **Contamination in the environment**

When a white cloth is dipped into a cup of red dye, it instantly taints the white fabric. The environment we live in can be like the red dye and our mind like the white cloth. As we are constantly exposed to the contamination of the world we live in, our mind can become blemished purely by being saturated by what's around us.

The negative messaging of mainstream media, hostile commentary on social media, trends in the culture, and declining standards of morality in our society all work to collectively exert a force on our thinking. And sometimes—or perhaps often?—there is a strategic plan at work to assault our thinking to influence our decision-making. John Tierney, co-author of *The Power of Bad*, notes that because our minds are prone to focus on the negative, for that reason media and political advertising can and do manipulate us by continually scaring us; 'market research shows that it's the way to get people's attention'.[78]

The Physical Effects of Negative Thinking

Clinicians call our recurring negative mindsets Automatic Negative Thoughts (ANT's). In these destructive patterns of worry and rumination, thinking negatively about ourself and the world, we become preoccupied with our perceived mistakes of the past, which results in judging ourselves harshly, criticism and emotional spikes of anger, guilt, sadness and shame.

Physiologically speaking, negative thinking causes chronic stress, which alters our brain's chemical make-up by depleting it of the naturally occurring feel-good neurotransmitters serotonin and dopamine. It also slows the production of protein used for new brain-cell formation, as it shrinks the brain but expands the brain's fear centre, the amygdala, and accelerates the brain's ageing process.

Further research by the University of Maryland School of Medicine proved that negative internal and external dialogue has a detrimental effect on our blood pressure and heart and alters the biochemistry of individual tissues throughout our bodies.[79]

In a new study, researchers at University College London in 2020 link repetitive negative thinking to cognitive decline, a higher number of harmful protein deposits in the brain, and consequently a greater risk of dementia.[80]

All of these conditions and responses to negative thinking are detrimental forces opposing our rise into our leadership potential.

You can't live a positive life with a negative mind.
—Anonymous

Realistic v. Negative Thinking

If we drive above the legal speed limit, we can be fined by the police, and if we jump off the roof of a house, gravity will pull us back to the earth. That's not being negative: that's realistic thinking based on the practicality and reality of the world we live in.

Realistic thinking has its place in our life, as it helps to prevent us from experiencing pain.

From our perspective in this chapter, negative thinking refers to those thoughts that attack fundamental issues of our identity, purpose, potential and ability. Negative thinking in this regard aims to keep us small and silent—wanting us to believe we are incapable of overcoming obstacles, experiencing personal growth or achieving great things.

The Need for Breakthrough Thinking

We are either empowering or disempowering ourselves with our thoughts.

World renowned author Dale Carnegie, known to millions for his iconic book *How to Win Friends and Influence People*, counsels that his first rule for cultivating a positive mental attitude is to 'fill your mind with thoughts of peace, courage, health and hope, *for our life is what our thoughts make it*' (my italics).[81]

To fulfil our leadership call, whether in the home, the workplace or the community, it is very likely that we will need to break through whatever limitations and negativity reside in our thinking.

Noting the importance to a leader of the power to persuade, Steve McVey, a former FBI hostage negotiator and current professor of Organisational Leadership at Purdue University, adds that often followers validate leaders on the basis of trust in the leader's superior thinking abilities.[82]

The environment around us can exert pressure to conform our thoughts to the status quo. Negative past experiences, inaccurate mental reasoning and unhealthy speculation can trap us inside a box we were never supposed to be in. These forces form strongholds in our thought life that can keep us captive. Strongholds are dominating thoughts and beliefs that rule over any opposing thought or belief. A thought stronghold occupies territory in our mind and will reject any other thought entering that territory, even if the stronghold thought is a lie and the new thought is truth. This occurs because in the realm of our mind, our perception is most definitely our reality. If we agree with it, if we give it power, it becomes truth to us.

Elephant trainers utilise the power of strongholds in the mind when training young elephants. As a baby, the elephant is tied to a tree with a strong, heavy-gauge chain, and despite the baby elephant's best efforts, it lacks the strength to break free from that chain. It is conditioned to think it cannot break away. As the elephant grows bigger, however, the heavy, bulky chain is replaced with progressively thinner rope. But the elephant never retests the 'truth' learnt from past experience and continues to live according to the inaccurate mental assumption that the tie around its leg is inescapable. Eventually, at the height of its power and strength, the fully grown, mighty elephant is held captive by a thin cord tied around its leg that does not even need to be attached to a post to be effective in immobilising it.[83]

The stronghold in the elephant's thinking is stronger than the piece of cord that holds it captive. It has learnt a pattern of thinking that becomes its own internal source of defeat, and any instinct to break free is deemed impossible.

Beyond being terribly sad, looked at objectively, it seems a ridiculous picture. A towering, monstrous, powerful beast held captive by a thin, unanchored cord. Yet that is a clear illustration of the power of strongholds in our thinking. If we cannot break the lie in our thinking, it becomes truth to us, and that truth defines our reality.

If we don't address it, we will always be captive. Whenever we try to chart a new course for our life, our embedded thoughts, perspectives and the strongholds in our mind will pull us back into the self-imposed jail cell and lock the door tight. A negative mind is the ultimate prison holding us back from entering our freedom and our potential.

If we carry a prevailing mindset that repeatedly tells us we're inadequate or going to fail, it's unlikely we will ultimately be victorious in any aspect of our life.

It is critical, therefore, to develop breakthrough-thinking patterns to deconstruct inaccurate thoughts we've allowed to determine who we are and our potential to impact the world around us.

Jamie, the team leader of the finance department of an automobile network of six car yards, coordinated the accounts-payable-and-receivable staff of four. The team met monthly; Jamie chaired the meeting, presenting an overview of updates and announcements for the month.

These occasions typically crippled Jamie with fear, as she had long believed people were secretly laughing at her whenever she spoke in public. She would not sleep the night before, was physically ill prior to the meeting and generally took the next day off to recover.

In reality, none of her team even suspected anything was wrong. They all felt Jamie spoke professionally, managed the meetings efficiently and even encouraged a laugh where appropriate. They thought she was a great team leader.

Until Jamie started to address the seed of these thoughts and reprogram her thinking, Jamie's inaccurate thought patterns would continue to produce these emotional and physical responses that were based on a complete lie.

Our life and our leadership can be transformed by taking ownership and authority over our thinking.

Little minds are tamed and subdued by misfortunes; but great minds rise above them.
—Washington Irving

The State of The Human Mind

So, why don't we just think positive thoughts? That would solve a lot of these thinking problems.

That would be nice, but unfortunately, a healthy mind filled with positive thoughts aligned to truth and self-belief is not the typical default state of the human mind. Dr. Jill Suttie, a psychologist and freelance journalist who writes for the *Greater Good* magazine published by UC Berkeley, describes the negativity bias: 'We humans have a propensity to give more weight in our minds to things that go wrong than to things that go right—so much so that just one negative event can hijack our minds in ways that can be detrimental to our work, relationships, health, and happiness'.[84]

Research by Roy F. Baumeister et al published in the *Review of General Psychology* (2001) produced clear and consistent evidence to justify their study title, 'Bad is Stronger Than Good', which argued that the negativity bias displayed by human adult psychology is 'one of the most basic and far-reaching psychological principles'.[85]

Other evidence suggests this negativity bias starts at a young age, even in infancy, where babies at the age of one begin to experience greater brain responses to negative stimuli. One study by eminent scientists, including an anthropologist from the Max Planck Institute in Leipzig, Germany, argued: 'We tentatively suggest that in typical development, a negativity bias might emerge as early as the second half of the first year'.[86]

Neuroscientific research has demonstrated that negative images produce a much stronger response in the electrical activity of the cerebral cortex than do positive or neutral images.[87]

Dr. Rick Hanson, author of *The New York Times* bestselling *Hardwiring Happiness*, notes that 'not only do negative stimuli trigger more neural activity, but research shows negativity is detected more quickly and easily. The region of the brain that regulates emotion and motivation uses about two thirds of its neurons to detect bad news'. 'The negativity bias of the brain gives us Velcro for bad experiences, but Teflon for good ones', he explains.[88]

Chemicals are released in our brain in direct response to every thought we produce, significantly influencing our mood and behaviour. Dopamine and serotonin provide us with a warm, *pat on the back* feeling, while cortisol, made by the adrenal glands, works with the brain to give us the negative, *slap on the wrist* emotions of stress and anxiety, such as when someone is spreading rumours about us in the office, or the car in our rear-vision mirror is too close to our rear bumper.

Unfortunately, our brain *loves* cortisol, which is why so many of us compulsively check our phone to see who has liked our Facebook post. The problem for a lot of us is that we develop a pattern of negativity because our brain responds more strongly to cortisol-related triggers.[89]

Psychologists Arien Mack and Irvin Rock's research debunked the assumption that our sensory organs—eyes, ears, etc.—consume all information presented to them equally and feed that information objectively to our brain. Their experiment involved asking viewers to watch a video and count how many times they see someone wearing a white shirt pass a ball. Immersed in the task, most subjects failed to see the gorilla walk right through the group. They were unaware of it until told to watch the video again.[90]

This research identified the concept of 'inattention blindness': that is, that it is our *focus* that determines what goes into the conscious mind, not what is actually in front of us. If our focus is negative to start with, that's all we will see in the world, at the exclusion of the positive.

As the saying goes *'most of us are like the rest of us'*, and for most of us, the default state of the human mind, as outlined in the 'negativity bias' above, is predisposed to orient toward the negative, expressed through such emotions as fear and anxiety. So don't think you're different from everyone else if you have a mind that doesn't want to cooperate, or seem overly helpful or kind to you. We can fall into the trap of looking at others and think 'it's different for them' or 'they've got it all together', assuming they have a mindset that lets them walk straight into victory. You would be surprised to learn how many people labelled as 'successful' have had to fight to overcome the battle between their ears.

Like Kim Perrell, a business entrepreneur and startup mentor who has had more than ten of the sixty startups she was an early investor in sell for over $500 million US.

Yet she admits that in the beginning of her career, 'I was terrified, broke and young. And everyone doubted me. But rather than focus on the thoughts of self-doubt, anxiety and worry I chose to press forward, block out their voices and believe in myself. Sometimes we act as though fear and self-doubt are real and true facts. Really, they're just emotions that are only as powerful as we make them. I stopped allowing those feelings to overwhelm me or distort my reality'.

She sold her most recent company for $235 million to one of the largest telecommunication companies in Asia and won the 2018 Women World Awards for Female Entrepreneur of the Year.[91]

Just as Kim proved, the negativity working against us in our own thinking, can be overcome.

Leadership Upgrade

The Danger of The Unrenewed Mind

Our mind is a stubborn, aggressive force, a constant to be reckoned with.

When left unattended and untrained, an unrenewed and negative mind runs rampant, dominating our life and creating seemingly insurmountable mountains and obstacles that overwhelm our perspective, while shutting down our hope, belief and vision.

The unrenewed mind's impact is like a constant supply of deadly poison being physically pumped into our body each day. Despite our best efforts to exercise and eat nutritious food, we're always going to be sick—operating below our best—until we turn off that toxic supply of chemicals entering our system. If our minds hold negative thinking, we will never be healthy.

A great story in *Entrepreneur* magazine explains how Michael was promoted to be National Sales Director of his company, yet couldn't shake the thought that he only got his promotion because no one else in sales was willing to relocate to the head office. His unrenewed thinking had the potential to derail him, literally push him out of the role he had deservedly earnt on the back of his hard work and performance. 'It was an extremely stressful period', he recalls. 'Was I was the right person for the job? These feelings stayed with me until I shifted my thinking and the conversation I was having with myself and developed a healthier self-narrative'.[92]

Left unaddressed, an unrenewed mind can prevent us from entering into what we are rightfully called to possess in our life. But Michael showed that it is possible to take control over self-destructive mindsets.

When our mind is capable of capturing and retaining truth or an inspired thought, and we can protect it from being squashed by negativity, we are able to build on that and move into our dreams and destiny.

Florence Nightingale, often known as 'the lady with the lamp', founded modern nursing and revolutionised the quality of healthcare during the 1800s.

From a young age in Britain, Florence wanted to become a nurse but for years was forbidden to do so by her family, who expected her to conform to the Victorian standards of marriage and childbearing. But refusing to relinquish her vision in her mind for over a decade, she finally was rewarded when her family conceded. They gave their permission, and she finally enrolled in nursing school at age thirty. She subsequently established the world-changing Nightingale Training School for Nurses in 1860.[93]

Breakthrough-Thinking Leaders

Breakthrough-thinking leaders understand that having excellence of thought life is not an option. It is an absolute must. If we think it, we can see and believe it. If we believe it, we can become it and we can reach it.

Forbes magazine highlights how crucial a tool mindset is for business startups. They note that to have the entrepreneurial mindset means being steadfastly committed to its vision, regardless of obstacles along the way—thus, seeing mistakes as an opportunity for growth, not as something to fear. This mindset, likewise, approaches problems from different angles to keep moving forward.[94]

When we begin to conquer the battlefield of the mind, we can imagine projects through to completion without the constant opposition of negative thinking.

> *The biggest wall you have to climb is the one you build in your mind: Never let your mind talk you out of your dreams . . . or become the greatest obstacle to success.*
> —Roy T. Bennett

Where others see the end, as breakthrough-thinking leaders, we see a beginning. When a setback causes others to stop, the resilience of our mind bounces us back to push forward again. Where fear and insecurity grind others to a halt, the overwhelming positivity and belief in our mind empower us to keep advancing.

Developing Breakthrough Thinking

To reach this level of breakthrough thinking, we need to train our mind to help us, by disciplining it to conform to truth, positive thought and accurate interpretation of external events.

UK-based leadership author and former business-news editor of *The Independent*, Roger Trapp, reports that while some people appear to be naturally resilient, able to cope with ups and downs, others take them very much to heart, becoming discouraged. Or they develop unhealthy habits in order to cope. But the good news is that resilience in our thinking can be learned.[95]

The Process of Mental Renewal & Resilience

We can learn mental resilience by understanding that rather than rely on changing our external circumstances to avoid stress, anxiety and negative thinking, we can develop our internal capacity to remain in a more consistent mental and emotional state.

The science of neuroplasticity refers to the brain's ability to adapt, update and change; in other words, we can create new connections and pathways between our neurons; this is something we can proactively encourage. Repetitive negative thinking creates pathways, but so do positive thinking patterns.[96]

Dr Caroline Leaf, a cognitive neuroscientist with a PhD in Communication Pathology and a BSc Logopaedics specialising in cognitive and metacognitive neuropsychology, over decades of research and experience has helped hundreds of thousands to learn how to use their mind to detox and grow their brain to succeed in every area of life. She explains: 'It takes 21 days to break down your thoughts and start the building process, but real neuroplasticity happens after 63 days'. Based on this science, she writes, 'Using the incredible power in our minds, we can persist and grow in response to life's challenges. We can take our thoughts captive and change the way we think, speak and act!'[97]

The Power of Choosing Thoughts

Understanding that we can proactively choose to insert any thought into our thinking, at any point in time, is crucial. When we begin to realise that we have the inherent power to substitute a positive, truthful, empowering thought for a negative, untrue, harmful thought and that we can control what we think, we are on the verge of a breakthrough.

Don't believe it's possible? Can you imagine how absurd a bright pink elephant would look walking through the lush green tropical jungle? With bananas in its ears? And a pair of fluffy slippers on all four feet? There you go, you just did it. You chose to insert that thought in your mind right then, at the expense of all others, and visualise that image. It's possible! Imagine what your life would be like if every hour you deliberately determined to think positive, accurate truths about yourself, other people, your future, and who you're taking with you. Your life would be changed.

Callan had his heart set on becoming a motivational speaker as a full-time profession.

He had a passion to help people, had taken courses on public speaking, motivation and personal coaching, and studied his craft diligently.

Callan had no public profile, to speak of. He was in debt and still lived with his parents. And his friends mocked him when he confided his dream. It's fair to say in Callan's life there was some fairly heavy opposition to reaching his plans and dreams.

But every morning Callan rose early and ran through a series of verbal affirmations to align his thinking with his goals. He declared his success over all obstacles, and that his purpose of helping others would be fulfilled. He affirmed that the circumstances around him would begin to change. Despite evidence to the contrary, he deliberately inserted thoughts of victory into his mental diet.

Eighteen months later Callan had his first booking as a motivational speaker, a presentation about road safety to a primary school. His most recent, however, was to a crowd of over 5,000 at a national network-marketing seminar, and Callan is booked solid for twelve months, with speaking engagements all over the world.

When we fill our mind with thoughts that work *for* us, not against us, we are more likely to break through. When our mind accepts it, our life can receive it.

Cultivating the Garden of Our Mind

Our mind is like a garden—capable of growing either beautiful flowers from seeds of positive, truthful thought, or ugly, destructive weeds from seeds of lies and negativity.

Your mind is the garden, your thoughts are the seeds, the harvest can either be flowers or weed.
—William Wordsworth

However, as with any natural garden, only one type of plant can grow in one space at one time. So, if these seeds of negativity have been sown and left unaddressed to grow and develop throughout our entire life, they have by now developed deep roots and abundant foliage that occupies significant territory in the garden of our mind. While occupying this space, it prevents any positive seed growing in that territory. It's a powerful picture of how a negative seed of thought can take root in our mind and aggressively expand in size and strength, creating a mental stronghold that dominates our thinking.

We may not realise where seeds in our thinking have come from, or when they were planted, however the type of seed we choose to sow, keep and cultivate in our mind, is entirely up to us.

If we created a beautiful flower garden at our home, we would not feel obligated to keep an ugly weed that grew up in the middle of it. We didn't plant it, we didn't pay for it, we didn't invite it, yet it has infiltrated our environment. We would rip it out and throw it away, lest it grow bigger and start to reproduce other weeds in our garden. We must take the same attitude when dealing with negative thoughts. They are not 'ours'. We don't 'own' them. They are just thoughts that have entered our consciousness. We are not obliged to keep them or accommodate them.

Never give a negative thought an inch
or it will take a mile.
—Matshona Dhliwayo

Jayde had always been a happy-go-lucky kid with a positive attitude, who felt that life was generally 'pretty awesome'. Being an only child, she spent most of her time with her parents, safe and happy in that environment. Then when she was eighteen, they divorced, an event that she knows 'planted a seed in my thinking that all romantic relationships were only temporary'. After a series of relationship breakups, she realised her own beliefs were a significant contributor to the failure. 'I was creating my own outcome before it had even happened, because that's what my thinking was telling me *would* happen, and that's what I was believing would eventuate'.

Jayde began to replace her negative thoughts and beliefs about relationships with positive ones, and her thought patterns have totally transformed in this area. She now enjoys a joyful long-lasting relationship. 'In the same way I used to predetermine my relationships would fail', she reveals, 'my spouse and I have predetermined this one will last forever'.

We need to be diligent with patrolling our thinking and disciplined in the maintenance of the garden of our mind. This process of uprooting the negative thoughts and sowing positive seed ultimately results in a new harvest in the faculty of our mind.

Chapter Nine – Breakthrough Thinking

Critical Areas of Thinking

There are two critical areas of thinking we need renewal and transformation in to succeed in our leadership journey.

i. Thoughts about other people

We need healthy, accurate thinking patterns is toward other people.

As leaders who function with breakthrough-thinking, we understand we are only ever ultimately leading people, not programs, organisations or projects.

Where we think that other people can't be trusted, don't work hard, just slow us down, aren't motivated, can't grow or learn new things, aren't as good as us or are out to take our job, then that type of thinking will severely negate our ability to raise a connected and productive team.

Where we think that other people have unique talents, can grow, are looking for a cause to join their heart to, have untapped potential, want to contribute and could strengthen our group, then that type of thinking is sure to produce a positive dynamic in the people around us.

Research in this area in the 1960s resulted in the creation of the term 'Pygmalion Effect', after the phenomenon of how teachers' pre-established expectations regarding the quality of their students were tangibly reflected in the student's grades. Subjects were divided into three groups, and their respective teachers were informed that the groups had been sorted into the highest-to-lowest academic achievers. Teachers of the most-talented group recorded positive thoughts about the quality of their students and held high expectations of their ability to learn. These students subsequently excelled. Conversely, teachers of the lowest-ranked academic students held assumptions these students would perform poorly. Unsurprisingly their class recorded the lowest results. The outcomes were remarkable, given that all the students in the study were actually of completely equal ability. The only variable was the belief the teacher held.[98]

This example highlights the power of a leader's influence on other people's ability to grow or remain limited. People will live up to, or down to, the expectations we, as leaders, hold of them and convey to them.

When people are lacking confidence, unsure of their identity, doubting their future success, struggling with negative self-talk or reliving past mistakes, sometimes the most powerful words they can hear from us are 'I believe in you'.

As breakthrough-thinking leaders, we set our minds on the potential inside of people, not just their problems, mistakes or shortcomings. We can't ignore the reality of where people are, their current understanding or behaviours, but we don't get stuck on the *now*. Instead, we progressively build a picture about *who they are becoming*, their latent talents and their possibilities.

Our mindset is always focused on equipping them to move past existing barriers and rise to the next level. This thinking dynamic requires a strategic mix of care, support, encouragement, challenge, discipline and correction.

ii. **Thoughts about ourself**

Our harshest critic can be the voice inside our head.

An overly inferior, limited, negative or critical self-image is a destructive ingredient in our make-up that will debilitate our capacity to succeed as a leader.

> *For as he thinks within himself, so he is.*
> —Proverbs 23:7

If our mind is dominated by thinking patterns that continually forecast our failure, replay previous errors, anticipate negative responses or dwell on our limitations, we are unlikely to function to our potential or convey a sense of inspiration or victory to those connected to us.

The Poisonous Effect of a Negative Self-Image

If we have not largely overcome our negative self-image, we will manifest this in our leadership. We will tend to seek answers to our identity questions from the very people we're trying to lead, instead of drawing from the conviction we've built inside us. When we have unresolved identity issues, our leadership will be tainted.

We will tend to draw energy and affirmation from others towards ourselves to address our own emotional needs. When this happens, our leadership becomes distorted, as we are more focused on meeting our individual needs than meeting the needs of the corporate objective.

For example, if we have a seed of self-rejection in our thinking and someone we know walks past us without saying hello, it immediately acts as confirmation of our internal belief that we are of low value. We assign a meaning to that event as further 'truth' to prove our preconceived mindset. Our mind is already geared up to filter and interpret data from the environment that reinforces the message our internal dialogue is repeating every hour, every week, every month of every year. This thinking pattern has become a well-worn and familiar path carved out from excessive and continual use.

If we're a person with a positive self-image and healthy thinking patterns, we likely interpret the same situation differently—that the other person simply didn't see us, that she had a lot on their mind, or that her lack of response doesn't affect our feelings about ourself or where we're heading in life, anyway. We would not interpret this event as a direct reflection on our value and identity.

The difference in response is not determined by each person's level of development, intelligence, title or position. The distinction lies under the surface, in the quality of their thinking.

Negative thinking about our image and identity will manifest in several ways, all of which attempt to hide and cover the fear, pain or lack we feel about our adequacy and validation as a person. These coping behaviours are typical attempts to compensate. A number of these coping mechanisms are listed below:

i. **Our identity becomes based on performance**

    Our predominant thinking becomes, *'If I achieve, I have value'*.

    Our focus on achievement and performance to cover over an inner insecurity will manifest in any one of several possible responses:

1. We continuously want to compete and win against another person—to come out 'on top'.

2. We avoid setting goals, targets or any measurable aimed-for outcomes. We can't fail if we don't have any goals to reach, and we will, therefore, avoid any scenario that provides quantifiable feedback informing us we weren't up to the task.

3. The fear of failure drives us to work and strive, sometimes maniacally, to avoid experiencing future defeat. This fear establishes a vicious cycle that can propel us into great achievement but is ultimately self-destructive, as our identity becomes based on what we do, not who we are.

4. We compare ourselves to others and wish we were like them, and had reached their achievements. We forego our unique talents and abilities, as we cannot see them in ourself. We hold a longing to literally be another person.

ii. **Our identity becomes based on popularity**

Our predominant thinking becomes, *'If I am popular, I have value'*.

In these situations, we create and maintain our popularity by making decisions to please people.

Pam and Lachlan, both in their mid-forties, were the proud parents of daughter Jess, now aged nineteen. Jess, a pleasant girl, nevertheless had developed a technique of getting her own way, and it played on Lachlan's sense of identity. Lachlan craved approval from almost everyone, after growing up with a largely absent father from the age of five on. Not having other role models, particularly male, it left him with a lack of validation as a person, man and father.

Since Jess's birth Lachlan and Pam had talked about setting guidelines and boundaries around basic parenting issues such as bedtime, foods to eat and length of playtime. While Pam easily adhered to these, Lachlan did not. When it came to enforcing a bedtime with Jess, if she reacted negatively with a bad attitude or tantrum, Lachlan realised that if he 'surrendered' and gave Jess what she wanted, she responded positively to him. Suddenly he found he had the power in his role as a parent to generate the approval from someone else he had always longed for.

Lachlan bent the rules to accommodate her demands or avoid a negative reaction. This pattern started with little things, like having to eat the vegetables on her dinner plate (Lachlan would slide Jess's onto his own plate when Pam wasn't watching). But as Jess grew up, the issues became more significant.

Pam was continually frustrated. 'It's not good for her in the long run', she would argue. 'How will she ever hold a job if she thinks she can just do whatever she likes?' She felt Lachlan and Jess were 'ganging up on her'. Lachlan, though, was only really concerned about keeping Jess's approval. He loved the idea of being the popular parent.

The impact of Lachlan's poor self-identity clearly influenced his parenting, and when Jess was sixteen, the consequences began to show. Her reactions to any attempts by Pam to set boundaries escalated into a daily battle of wills. 'Dad doesn't make me do any of this stuff', Jess would argue before storming off.

Pam resented Lachlan for his lack of unwillingness to stand up to Jess. Jess also began regularly taking money from Lachlan's wallet, knowing he would never confront her.

As the family descended into unrest, it ultimately fractured. Exasperated, Pam left, reasoning to Lachlan that 'I'm by myself in this house anyway' before she walked out the door. Jess was living her own life, cycling to the next fun event or party and treating her dad with little respect—largely as a bank to fund her activities.

Lachlan, for all his unintentional ineptness, was left alone to reflect.

Months later, during some informal counselling, Lachlan acknowledged his role in the breakdown: his need to be 'liked' had provided him some temporary popularity with Jess, but he had not created an environment that facilitated her growth in character and maturity, or provided support to his wife.

Children 'liking' a parent may fulfil the parent's emotional need, but the leadership mandate to raise a mature person equipped for adult life is unlikely to be fulfilled.

As a breakthrough-thinking leader, our mindset is not to gain popularity, but to fulfill our purpose. We need to be secure and robust enough in our self-identity to lead without prejudice or undue self-interest, in the best interests of those in our care.

If you want to make everyone happy,
don't be a leader, sell ice cream.
—Steve Jobs

---

iii. Our identity becomes based on position

Our predominant thinking becomes, *'If I'm the boss, I have value'*.

In this scenario, we rely on our position, role or title to reassure ourselves we have value.

By merely pulling rank, we can always shut down an argument or a difference of opinion. It removes any obligation on our part to demonstrate leadership through influence and relationship, discuss an issue, listen to others, take responsibility for our actions, explain or communicate decisions or engage and inspire people.

We can always 'win' by using our position, and we feel insecure without it.

As a leader with a healthy self-identity, we will train, prepare and make room in the environment for others to grow and function. However, if we have a negative self-image and are reliant on our title and position, we can misinterpret others' development and keen participation. Even when their actions align with our group's objectives, we perceive them as a threat, ensuring we keep ourselves at the top of the pecking order. We may do this even if it slows the progress of the team to achieve its goal.

iv. Our identity becomes based on power

Our predominant thinking becomes, *'If I can make people do what I want, I have value'*.

When we use power in an unhealthy manner, with a twisted motivation, we can:

- threaten with coercive power,

- manipulate with information power,

- control situations through connection power,

- entice with reward power

- intimidate with perceived power

- or direct with our expert power

When we're leaders with a healthy self-identity, we do not rely on our power over others to make them do what we want. Instead, we are secure enough in our own identity to encourage, support and empower people to grow and contribute.

We would not presume to manipulate, control or violate a person's own will, even if their choices are contradictory to the ones we would wish for them and do not support the interests of the group.

We may still issue consequences in these cases, but only to protect the interests of the group, not just for the sake of demonstrating our power.

CHAPTER TEN

Self-Governance

*Self—the identity, character, or essential qualities
of any person or thing*

Govern—to exercise continuous sovereign authority over.
To be a leader in anyone else's world, we first need to be a leader of our own. We can't govern anything around us until we govern what's in us.

The capacity to govern ourself is one of the most important qualities we can ever develop. This is because the most important and challenging person we'll ever have to lead is ourself.

Who is fit to govern others? He who governs himself.
—Augustus William Hare

Self-control and self-governance remains a much sought-after, but elusive reality. Eighty per cent of New Year's resolutions fail, and general efforts to change our behavior fail more than half the time.[99]

Our lives are all governed by something. And what governs us governs our leadership.

Who we are in private is who we are as a leader in public. *How we live is how we lead.*

Leadership coach Dave Ferguson, author of *Hero Maker: Five Essential Practices for Leaders to Multiply Leaders*, draws the distinction between two key forces—selfishness and selflessness—that govern leaders and leadership motivation:

i. 'Selfishness'—indicates we are most concerned about ourself: our image, performance, and desires

ii. 'Selflessness'—entails being more concerned about others[100]

Self-governing leaders pay attention to their thoughts, rather than allowing decision-making to be unduly influenced by emotions; they monitor and have awareness of their behavior; manage time effectively; demonstrate accountability and integrity of character; build relationships and teams and display consistency.[101]

Diminishing the influence of a self-focused agenda enables us as leaders to pursue others-focused goals and a mission that is bigger than just ourselves.

Author Carey Nieuwhof, whose leadership podcast has over twelve million downloads worldwide, explains that all leaders are ambitious and have goals, but the key question a leader must ask is, *What is my motivation*? 'Because if you don't ask it, I promise everyone else around you will. Great leaders aren't driven by personal ambition, they're driven by the mission. Ambition is a terrible substitute for mission'.[102]

What masters our heart, and what we ultimately end up serving, is what we love the most. When our life is continually conditioned to satisfy the demands of our selfishness, it becomes increasingly difficult to reconfigure any of our thoughts, beliefs or actions to contradict that priority.

Marcel Schwantes, a leadership coach whose work on human-centred workplaces that result in high-performing cultures has been featured on CNBC, Forbes, and Time, hits the nail on the head: 'Leadership is a *heart* matter. If the heart is not right, your leadership isn't going to be right. The heart of a leader has to be focused on serving others first. . . . It's a heart that is driven by service and the overarching life philosophy of 'How many lives can I impact for the better?''[103]

Winnie was the manager of the communications department of a regional government water board. Her team found her pleasant enough to work for, but were resigned to the fact that in her ceaseless practice of self-promotion Winnie would claim credit for any work the team presented to senior management. A deep-seated resentment and an agreed-upon culture amongst the team members to 'do the bare minimum' resulted.

Janelle Spense of Centennial, a successful executive-recruitment company since 1975, argues about the importance—even for those already achieving success—of leadership that is others-focused, as opposed to self-focused: 'From a distance, the results may look the same, but to those who are close to you, the chasm is enormous'.[104]

If we are not able to redirect selfish ambition, our leadership will be distorted, our goals limited. Our leadership walk effectively becomes all about us, and 'we' become the total focus of our assignment and calling.

We cannot lead unselfishly if we are connected to and pursuing a selfish purpose.

Past President of the American Psychoanalytic Association Prudy Gourguechon, now a sought-after media commentator and business advisor after thirty-five years of experience as a psychiatrist and organisational leader, has developed a model of leadership assessment that spells out the fundamentals of character. She gives great weight to self-control as an essential leadership trait, but unfortunately, it rarely shows up in the corporate world on the list of what makes a good leader: 'Consideration of leadership qualities tends to look at behaviour and results, rather than character'.[105]

However, she cautions that 'a pattern of behavior that betrays a lack of self-control should always be seen as a serious problem with significant personal and business consequences'.

Without the maturity to restrain an extreme self-focus, then by default we live, and lead, selfishly.

Identifying Selfishness in Our Life

Selfishness, as we all know, involves being concerned excessively or exclusively with oneself, regardless of the needs or feelings of others.

Selfish behaviour is often the result of immaturity or the ability to manage our emotions and take full responsibility for our actions across all the range of environments on a daily basis.

It means generally, in regards to character, we have not fully developed or grown, and lack wisdom, insight, and emotional stability.

Maturity appears when we start to worry more about others than about ourselves.
—Albert Einstein

Online neuroscience magazine *Exploring Your Mind* defines emotional immaturity as 'a condition where a person hasn't given up the desires or fantasies of their childhoods. These desires and fantasies have to do with them being the centre of the universe'.[106]

Adam was a great dad. He loved his two young teenage daughters, and they him. But the whole family knew he was essentially still 'one of the kids' that needed looking after. He forgot important appointments, never took ownership of the household administrative responsibilities like arranging insurance, and couldn't ever stick at anything to see it through. The 'hard'-parenting stuff, he avoided—not enforcing discipline or setting standards at home. He was a lovely guy, but had just never matured into a fully functioning and responsible adult, meaning Margaret had to assume a lot of the heavy lifting on the home front. This always created a slight imbalance in the relationship and tension in the home.

Selfishness and immaturity can manifest in a range of behaviours—in the work, home or community environment. It's possible to move from one end of the spectrum to another quickly. For example, we may handle the demanding pressure of public office with poise and display grace and patience to staff and the public, yet complain to our wife about the quality of her home-cooked meal.

As a quick self-assessment as you read, you may like to rate yourself on the scenarios below. I've scored towards the lower end of all of these indicators at various points of my personal life and leadership journey. I realise that it doesn't make me a bad person, it just makes me human. But taking a quick assessment has provided a reality check at times about where my heart and motivations were in certain situations.

One area I've had to grow in (and am still growing in!) was my tendency to be very task oriented. So when I'm focused on completing a task or project, I potentially start to tune out people and events around me that need me to be present and involved. Instead, I can be selfishly engrossed in the tunnel vision of achieving my goal.

Or sometimes I'm very aware of how I am communicating with others, really covering what I'm saying with great clarity and listening like a pro. Other days I leave large gaps in the information I'm sharing and just expect people to read my mind or understand why we're doing something! But I'm making progress. Here is the quick self-assessment 'test':

Measure your responses on a scale of 0 (strongly disagree) to 10 (strongly agree) to these statements:

- You're a poor communicator: do you ever listen to anyone? are you open and transparent, or do you like to keep people guessing?

- You use people: is there a trail of discarded bodies in your wake? Do you influence people to do things that only you get the benefit from?

- You abuse the authority of your position: do you use 'insider influence and knowledge' to profit yourself?

- You live by your emotions: do you get offended easily?

- You promote yourself, not others: do you claim credit for others' efforts?

- You never apologize—can you say *sorry*? Or is there no need, seeing as you are never wrong?

- You don't take responsibility: are you happy for others to take the fall for consequences arising from your decisions?

- Your principles are flexible in a way that ensures you benefit: are you happy to adjust your values to get a reward?

- You are only concerned with results, not people: are you prepared to jeopardise reaching a goal to consider the welfare of someone else?

- You have no impulse control: do you fly off the handle at the slightest trigger?

- You spend irresponsibly: do you buy things you don't need or can't afford? throw away valuable things? Are you in debt and never get out of debt?[107]

Are We Naturally Selfish or Unselfish?

The 2016 *Annual Review of Psychology* reminds us that as far back as nearly four centuries ago, Thomas Hobbes proposed that self-interest is the most fundamental human motivation.[108]

Research has also shown, however, that this behaviour is not fixed: people can rise above the inclination to be self-serving.

Neuroscience research into determining behaviour on the selfish-selfless spectrum published in the *Frontiers of Psychology* journal concluded that human behaviour can demonstrate both selfish and selfless attributes, and that individuals and groups are capable of shifting behaviour on the spectrum in response to social and cultural experiences.[109]

The choice to act selfishly or unselfishly will come before us in many situations in our role as leaders—at home, in the community or workplace—every day.

Sarah was the senior manager of a government department, a role she had held for over ten years.

One of Sarah's team members came to her with evidence linking elected officials and directors of the department to a land deal that was a serious conflict of interest. Sarah told her to leave it with her, she would take appropriate action. Based on her lucrative executive salary, Sarah was accustomed to a luxury lifestyle that included a top-of-the-range vehicle, parcel of countryside land, a renovated homestead and the ability to send her two sons to the best private schools in the region. In another eight years she would retire, accessing her sizable superannuation, able to pursue her passion for travel, which she had sacrificed by working long hours to climb the corporate ladder.

When a former colleague raised issues of probity involving elected representatives and high-ranking executives, Sarah had watched as that staff member was promptly 'restructured' out of the organisation. She didn't want to suffer the same fate and jeopordise her future lifestyle. As you may have guessed, the information she received never went anywhere but to the trash.

The Rise of Self-Focused Behaviour in Society

While we may have the potential to act selflessly, statistics indicate that as a global community, self-absorbed lifestyles are on the rise—as a society in general, we are failing to control, or attempt to, the selfish traits of our human nature.

The implications of this trend are that more people will move into leadership roles in which their approach reflects this selfishness.

These indicators include the following:

Individualism—A study published in *Psychological Science* in 2017 suggests over the past several decades a worldwide trend that people are becoming more individualistic than collectivistic (how community and family oriented we are).[110]

Self-importance—Research involving U.S. college students found that the proportion describing themselves as 'an important person' spiked from 12 per cent in the 1950s to 80 per cent in the 1980s.[111]

Lying—In one study 60 per cent of participants reported that they told on average two to three lies during a ten-minute conversation. Another study found that where 60 per cent of survey respondents reported telling no lies, 92 per cent admitted they actually had lied in the previous week.[112]

Divorce—The rate has more than doubled, increasing from 0.8 per 1,000 persons in 1965 to 2 in 2017.[113]

The most commonly reported reasons in a study of fifty-two divorced individuals were infidelity, domestic violence and substance use. All issues related to self-focus and self-control.[114]

Addiction—Addiction is increasingly becoming a worldwide trend in lifestyle, prevalent in rich and poor countries alike and now regarded as a major public-health problem. Besides alcohol and drugs, other addictions, including computer games, gambling, sex and food, also have severe consequences on health of the individual and society.[115]

The American Addiction Centre says there are two possibilities regarding addictive behaviours: 1) a complete loss of behavior control; or 2) a decreased ability to control cravings for pleasure.[116] Both evidence a lack of self-governance. Here's a breakdown:

Leadership Upgrade

i. **obesity**—Worldwide obesity has nearly tripled since 1975.[117]

ii. **pornography**—In Poland, researchers report a 310 per cent increase in the proportion of population who used online pornography from 2004 to 2016.[118]

In America now, 35 per cent of all internet downloads are related to pornography.[119]

iii. **alcohol**— The *Lancet Medical Journal* published research showing that individual alcohol consumption worldwide has soared, increasing by 70 percent over the last thirty years, with further rises predicted through to 2030.[120]

iv. **drugs**—The United Nations Office on Drugs and Crime reported a 30 per cent increase in drug use worldwide between 2009 and 2018.[121]

v. **gambling**—The UK Gambling Commission published their 2017 report, estimating that the number of individuals in the UK with a serious gambling problem had risen by more than one third in the previous three years.[122]

Reviewing these figures would suggest that our ability, or desire, to move away from self-serving desires and behaviours is declining.

How we live is how we lead. If we want to be a self-governing, others-focused leader, we need to start by reviewing the behaviours we display in our private life.

The Impact of Selfish Leadership

In the family environment, those with egoistic motivations tend to provide low levels of support to their partner, while unhealthily self-focused parents can use children to serve their own selfish needs or can be so self-obsessed their children become invisible.[123]

Audrey, a good-natured, seventeen-year-old, was selecting a graduation dress with her mum, who held one up, exclaiming, 'I found the perfect dress for you!' It was red-and-white striped, and Audrey hated it. She reluctantly tried it on. 'I love it!' her mum exclaimed. Audrey hesitated. Briefly displaying her reluctance, she instantly drew her mum's agitated reaction. Audrey quickly conceded the point, as usual, to keep the peace, but her inability to have any differing views than what her mum imposed on her continued to frustrate her. On graduation night, when her date raised an eyebrow and commented, 'Red stripes?' she burnt with anger inside.[124]

Marriage and Family Therapist Dr. Karyl McBride, a twenty-eight-year veteran of private and public practice, talks about the effect of an extreme case of self-focus, narcissistic personality disorder, NPD. As she has seen in her private and public life for over twenty-eight years, 'Being raised by a narcissistic parent is emotionally and psychologically abusive and causes debilitating, long-lasting effects to children'.[125]

Corporate-leadership trainer Ken Blanchard, who in 2005 was inducted into Amazon's Hall of Fame as one of the top twenty-five bestselling authors of all time, has studied the negative impact of self-oriented leaders in the workplace and warns, 'If you want to have robotic employees who only do what they're told to do and what they're rewarded to do, then keep putting controlling managers in front of them', Blanchard states.[126]

Leadership strategist and culture coach Dan Pontefract, notes it's the selfish leaders who focus on power, pay and profit that create collateral damage in employees, customers, partners and society in general.[127]

In Australia, former General Manager of the charity Guide Dogs Victoria, Sandro Cirianni, misused $210,000 of the organisation's money, creating fake invoices to pay for the installation of a pool in his home, restaurant meals and personal items, despite earning a $169,000 salary. Remarkably, he was named the state's not-for-profit manager of the year in 2015. In his awards acceptance speech Cirianni explained, rather revealingly, 'I really enjoy working collaboratively with people so that we can get the best out of them for the benefit of the whole organisation'.[128]

A healthy reminder to us that the apparently well-meaning, even celebrated behavior of leaders can mask an underlying contradictory motive.

The selfishness of leaders can impact society. The greed of self-focused financial-institution leaders sparked the 2007 financial crisis, which spread from the United States, where the household wealth of the nation plummeted $12–$14 trillion, to the rest of the world. Veteran Wall Street journalist Robert Lenzer described the attitude of bank and financial industry leaders contributing to the crisis as having such 'rotten hubris, such selfish, self-aggrandizing drives that they act like primitive warriors from a more violent time'. A crisis that, he noted, has impacted generations to come.[129]

Associate professor at Ovidius University Constanta in Romania, Dr Claudia Ioana, agrees. In her paper titled, 'Greed and the Global Financial Crisis', she highlights that ultimately, the unscrupulous tactics significantly contributed to the collapse of the financial system. Proof that the consequences of *'uncontrolled greed can lead us into a deep and long-lasting economic recession'.*[130]

How the degree of greed displayed by bank directors and the unscrupulous tactics significantly contributed to the collapse of the financial system.

The Impact of Un-Selfish Leadership

In contrast to the negative impact of selfish leadership, executive coach Marcel Schwantes, who has 1.5 million readers every month globally, declares that 'In all my research to find the most remarkable leadership style that impacts both people and profit, I have concluded that nothing can match 'servant leadership', which focuses on others first'.[131]

In any environment, be it work, family or community, if we practice selflessness, inspiring trust and confidence, we will help draw out the potential in others because they feel they will be supported and protected. I read this following story in the newspaper and kept it as a great example of a journey towards selfless leadership in the home.

Like any father, Matt was proud to be a dad, ecstatic about having a beloved newborn, but nevertheless used work as an excuse to stay away from the chaos of evening childcare. 'Easier to let the wife deal with the whiff of nappies and screaming baby', he reasoned.

Matt's wife, Laura, also working, was left to handle full-time caring duties plus her job, and before long this strain took its toll. She turned to Matt for help. 'But I didn't give it', Matt reflected later. 'I may be a dedicated member of my workforce. But when it came to being a parent and husband, I fell short'.

Twelve months passed. After an incident of projectile vomit by the baby in the car Laura reached her breaking point. In a tear-filled plea, she blurted out that she wasn't coping and complained how frustrated she was by Matt's focus on work.

Crushed by a wave of guilt, Matt promised to change, regardless of his love for the calm of the office. And he followed through. He right away adjusted his focus to be much more involved at home. Things improved, so much so that after their second child, Matt made the decision to become a full-time dad to support Laura's skyrocketing career. 'The stress of both of us having careers and two toddlers just wasn't worth it', he reflected. 'In fact, I'm not sure our marriage would have survived'.[132]

Leadership—The Amplifier of Our Character

Clearly, leading unselfishly produces great benefits to our family, organisation and society. This applies whether we are a parent, a CEO, a school student or member of a volunteer group.

So why don't we just act unselfishly?

The reason why we don't, and can't, just flick the switch and act unselfishly as a leader is because the role of leadership doesn't change who we are, it only amplifies what's already in us.

It could be said that the way people use the power of leadership depends on their pre-existing values.

In other words, if we're self-focused as a person, we'll be self-focused as a leader.

Canadian billionaire businessman Stewart Butterfield, CEO and co-founder of Slack, a corporate communications software used by over 750,000 companies, quipped about being a leader and acquiring power, 'It just makes you more of who you already were'.[133]

Chapter Ten – Self-Governance

Typically, a leadership role carries a unique level of power and authority, not accessible to us until we move into it, even if it's informal or unwritten, such as becoming a dad in a family.

Former US president Lyndon B. Johnson, holder of one of the most powerful positions in the world, is quoted as saying, 'Power always reveals. When you have enough power to do what you always wanted to do, then you see what the guy always wanted to do'.

How did Darlene Bradley use her position as mayor of Davenport, Florida? She was found guilty in 2017of using dead people's handicap-parking permits to park at City Hall and placed on a six-month good-behaviour bond.

Organisational psychologist, TED speaker, four times *New York Times* best-selling author Adam Grant has been recognized as one of the world's ten-most-influential management thinkers. He states that 'how you use authority reveals your character: Selfish leaders hoard power for personal gain. Servant leaders share power for social good. And the ultimate test of character for people in power is how they treat people who lack it. Gaining influence and authority frees us up to act on our real wishes and show our true colors'.[134]

Any immaturity and selfish ambition that is in us is amplified when we assume leadership roles.

The Impact of Power

While leadership reveals our true character and motives, the associated power has additional consequences.

In a 1972 article, 'Does Power Corrupt?' David Kipnis, in the *Journal of Personality and Social Psychology*, examines the five negative effects 'control of power' has in a simulated organisational setting with twenty-eight undergraduates, concluding that leaders are typically endowed with power, and power can corrupt.[135]

Research has shown that this power increases the likelihood that people will engage in moral hypocrisy, use people and satisfy their own needs and goals ahead of the group's best interest.[136]

Firstly, because the temptations of power are such that it increases goal-oriented behavior and amplifies the tendency of self-focused goals to yield self-interested behavior. Secondly, because a leadership position typically affords us a higher rank in the hierarchy, access to more resources through an increased delegation of authority, a safer tenure, the admiration of followers, freedom to act on our own, unchecked ambition and a sense of entitlement.[137]

In 1995 Slovak Prime Minister Vladimir Meciar, through a peculiar set of circumstances, temporarily also became the country's president. He used his dual positions to conveniently issue a presidential pardon to himself for the crime of kidnapping and murdering the former president's son.

Dacher Keltner, a UC Berkeley professor in the Department of Psychology, draws an interesting analogy: 'When you give people power, they actually begin to exhibit behaviour similar to neurology patients with brain damage. While it takes a lot of empathy and social intelligence in the process of gaining power, it is a very easy thing to lose once the power is obtained'.[138]

Once power is achieved, leaders are typically, sometimes intoxicatedly, highly motivated to protect it, and evidence shows they are willing to act unethically, at others' expense, and not in the group interests, to keep it.[139]

Studies in the workplace by Jon Maner and Nicole Mead published in 2010 in the *Journal of Personality and Social Psychology* demonstrated that where a subordinate had opportunity to outshine the leader and potentially take over that role, the latter would willingly sacrifice the good of the group and isolate those potential threats in order to prevent threatening alliances from being formed—all as a means of protecting his or her own power.[140]

To do this, dominant leaders withhold valuable information, exclude skilled group members from discussion and assign skilled members to less-influential roles.[141]

In organisations with lower levels of formal authority structure, such as political parties and community networks, the jostling amongst members to stay at the top of the heap may be even more pronounced.

Associate Professor Morela Hernandez of Virginia University conducts research into how organisations enable self-serving behaviour. She notes that leaders may engage in 'motivated reasoning' to help justify their self-serving behaviour and convince themselves of the fairness of their actions. This reasoning in turn facilitates ongoing self-serving behavior.[142]

With specific focus on the political realm, clinical psychologist Dr. Leon Seltzer, a long-time blogger for *Psychology Today*, whose posts have received almost 44 million views, notes that ironically, despite professing steadfast ethical values, self-focused politicians can be viewed as 'moral relativists', in that what they adamantly deem immoral for others is yet somehow acceptable for them.

In his article 'Narcissism: Why It's So Rampart in Politics: Narcissist Politicians Don't Serve the People, They Serve Themselves', he notes what an exaggerated sense of entitlement 'narcissist–politicians' demonstrate in augmenting their income through insider trading and investments. He describes the drive of many politicians, in particular, for power, prestige, status and authority: 'So, nothing if not opportunistic, they take from public and private coffers alike whatever they think they can get away with. And given their grandiose sense of self, they're inclined to believe they can get away with most anything'.[143]

Australian politician Eddie Obeid was a member of the New South Wales state legislative council from 1991 to2011. Investigations in 2012 into Obeid's conduct found he misused his position as a member of Parliament in relation to café leases, and 'corruptly [lobbied] his former colleagues to gain lucrative concessions over café leases at Circular Quay that were secretly owned by his family'.

He was expelled from the party in May 2013, charged with misconduct in public office and in 2016 sentenced to five years in jail.

The NSW Court of Criminal Appeal dismissed his subsequent appeal, on the basis that 'it was inconceivable that a politician of sixteen years' standing who had been a Minister for four years did not know that his duty was to serve the public interest and that he was not elected to use his position to advance his own or his family's pecuniary interests'.[144]

Yale researcher Ryan Carlson describes the use of a mental coping strategy by self-focused leaders to satisfy their own positive self-image, while almost denying the action ever took place or that it was wrong: 'Most people strive to behave ethically, but people sometimes fail to uphold their ideals. In such cases, the desire to preserve a moral self-image can be a powerful force and not only motivate us to rationalise our unethical actions, but also 'revise' such actions in our memory'.[145]

Rather than serving the people that elected them, they use their position of privilege to manipulate outcomes that ultimately benefit only themselves.

A 2013 article in the *American Psychological Association* examining 'The Essential Tension between Leadership and Power' encouraged 'avoiding the selection of leaders who displayed too strong a hunger for power' in a bid to reduce the potential for corruption.[146]

Transitioning Away from Self-Focused Behaviour

Moving closer toward others-centred selflessness has been a pursuit of humanity since time began.

The ability to govern the negative, unhealthy, dark aspects of our nature that seek to promote our own needs at the cost of someone else's well-being remains a critical issue.

> *Like a city whose walls are broken through*
> *is a person who lacks self-control.*
> —Proverbs 25:28

The main problem we face is that it's very difficult to *combat ourself with ourself.* Trying to change ourself with our own self is like trying to pull ourselves up by our shoelaces.

We can change our location, job, image, name or even our spouse, all relatively easily and quickly, but we can never simply just change the nature of our self-life.

Three key strategies to develop our maturity and governance of our self-life are listed and discussed below:

1. Applying self-discipline
2. Engaging with a mentor
3. Connecting to a higher vision

1. Applying Self-Discipline

The Collins Dictionary describes self-discipline as 'the ability to control yourself and to make yourself work hard or behave in a particular way without needing anyone else to tell you what to do'.

Our ability to say 'no' to those negative or extreme self-focused patterns and 'yes' to a selfless set of behaviours is an important part of the journey towards self-governance.

Self-Discipline and Self-Governance

The practice of self-discipline is a pathway to developing self-governance; however, they are not the same thing.

While we can conform our behaviour to meet the requirements of a self-discipline regime or to reach a specific goal, once the program finishes or the goal is reached, we have not necessarily undergone any inward transformation of our priorities, preferences or lifestyle choices, but have only demonstrated the ability to behave in a particular manner. It's possible we might simply revert to our past behaviour and patterns.

Discipline imposed from the outside eventually defeats when it is not matched by desire from within.
—Dawson Trotman

Self-governance happens when the values and purpose we are pursuing become intrinsic—applied voluntarily because of our conviction. This internal dynamic creates a renewal in our character and a realisation about 'who we are'.

Research from England showed that 80 per cent of ex-smokers now identifying themselves as nonsmokers were less likely to start again than those who still thought of themselves as smokers.[147]

The internal transformation is crucial to a transition from self-discipline to self-governance.

> *It is not the mountain we conquer, but ourselves.*
> —Sir Edmund Hilary

Key Principles of Self Discipline

i. Self-discipline activates the principle of alignment in our life, where our thinking, emotions, beliefs and body all start working together to reach a common goal.

If we've already predetermined we're going to keep going, our mind is not able to gain traction with thoughts of giving up. Our body is not able to dictate to us what time we get out of bed if we've set the alarm and decided to jump out of bed as soon as it goes off. When our mind, emotions and body are aligned, in agreement, the self is forced to conform to the majority vote. It is unable to find an entry point to exert influence on our decision-making.

Thirty-six-year-old Eva loved her deserts, chocolate and junk food. Unfortunately, she was also overweight. So she decided to change her diet. Although having quite a physical, mental and emotional dependency on fatty and sugary foods, she committed to a diet of wholesome nutrition. To help, she threw out all the junk food she had stored in cupboards at home and drawers at work, teamed up with an accountability partner and always drove routes that didn't go past her favorite takeout restaurants or bakeries.

Her self-discipline helped her move from unhealthy impulses and attachments and establish new habits that saw her lose 12 kilograms in just four months.

ii. **Self-discipline builds our habits, and habits build our lifestyle**

Either our habits will master us, or we will master them.

'We are what we repeatedly do. Excellence, then, is not an act but a habit' is a familiar phrase that provokes thought.

For example, if we discipline ourselves to habitually study for an hour at 7 p.m., it's less likely that we will waste that hour unproductively or be led into harmful behaviours.

The undisciplined are slaves to moods, appetites and passions.
—Stephen Covey

---

iii. **When we commit to self-discipline, we take ownership of our present situation and future growth.**

When we assume responsibility for our thinking, habits and priorities, we have started the transition from victim to victor. We are no longer content to apportion blame or justify our actions by the situation or circumstances, but assume ownership to change it.

2. Engaging with a Mentor

When we engage with a mentor, we gain access to an entire dimension of experience, wisdom, support and feedback we would not have if journeying alone.

Lucy Lloyd, the co-founder and CEO of Mentorloop, a company that strategically matches mentors with mentees says, 'The right connections can change your life. Leadership mentoring is a tried and trusted method for developing the best leaders of tomorrow'.[148]

Mentoring relationships often serve to draw out the potential in us and inspire us to pursue our dreams.[149]

Amy graduated from college with top marks in her communications degree and enrolled in the graduates mentoring program. She explains:

'I was bracing myself, expecting my mentor to storm in and start telling me what jobs to apply for and how to get ahead, but instead, my mentor, Suzy, just asked me a lot of questions, like, 'What are you passionate about?' and 'What do you value in life?' It was literally nothing to do with work.

Through that process I zeroed in on my interest in training and education and have since been hired by a corporation that focuses on teaching financial skills and budgeting to low-socioeconomic sections of the community.

My mentor helped me understand who I am and where my motivations lay.

Mentors can instil confidence and equip us with capabilities to overcome barriers. As they share their successes and mistakes, they become a 'tangible, humble and accessible example of what success can look like'.[150]

When we enjoy the personal touch of a mentor we can talk to, share with and draw from, our growth increases exponentially. Evidence from the workplace shows that managers' productivity increases by 88 per cent with mentoring and training, versus 24 per cent with training alone.[151]

Mary Abbajay, author of *Managing Up: How to Move Up, Win at Work, and Succeed with Any Type of Boss*, confirms the corporate world has grasped the positive impact mentoring has on their competitive edge and people development, with 71 per cent of Fortune 500 companies now adopting active mentoring programs. In return, they get higher levels of employee engagement, retention and knowledge sharing.[152]

In the community setting, mentoring has been shown to provide positive civic outcomes, such as increased social responsibility and socially responsive leadership.[153]

A key contributor to the power of mentoring lies in the accountability established, where the mentee is open about feelings and behaviours, allowing the mentor to speak into those areas.

American company Accountable2U's entire business is based on the effectiveness of accountability in developing maturity; as well, it's able to 'break habits and conquer addictions'. The company software can 'track your internet browsing, device activity, apps used, and even your location history'. They suggest, 'Perhaps you have a pattern of behaviour or mode of thinking that sabotages your success or negatively affects others. Being accountable to others can help you become aware of your blind spots and challenge you to get out of your old routine'.[154]

Mentoring can contribute to our development and maturing of character, where we can move away from self-focused behaviours toward a higher level of self-governance.

3. Connecting to a Higher Vision

The vision we are following is the key driver of our life and leadership.

When we connect to a vision that is bigger than our immediate wants and needs, its associated sense of assignment or mission calls us up out of our self-focus to a higher plane.

It's difficult to become more others-focused if everything in our life revolves around ourselves. Our ambition to be richer. Our need to be more powerful—wanting more possessions, consumed with satisfying ourself.

Dr Jim Taylor, an internationally recognized authority on the psychology of performance, parenting, technology, and popular culture warns that many people in this generation get trapped in the self-focused culture of winning, status, power, appearance and conspicuous consumption, which don't actually bring happiness or meaning to our life.[155]

Becoming less self-focused, though, is a challenge for anyone. Our life, while it may be causing us unhappiness, is nonetheless familiar and comfortable, with our habits ingrained. That's why a vision and a purpose greater than ourselves is a powerful catalyst we can connect with, allowing its momentum to pull us forward, while drawing us away from self-focused routines and priorities.[156]

Leaders of Cone Healthcare in North Carolina created a vision for putting the needs of their patients first, ahead of all other organisational priorities and staff's personal concerns or preferences. The vision soon ignited new inspiration and the passion to set, and then to realize, bold goals. Re-energised staff worked to disengage from old mindsets and aligned their thinking and actions with the values of prioritising patient care, removing redundant activities and traditional approaches that didn't serve the vision. It resulted in decreased employee turnover, increased employee engagement and a decline in patient readmissions.[157] The clarity of a vision allows us to say 'yes' to what matters, and 'no' to what doesn't.

When we connect to a vision that's bigger than ourselves, we start to serve the values inherit in that vision, and this drives a change in our behaviour.

John's vision for his family of wife and three children was that they would be a close-knit, loving family, with a priority on connecting and building healthy and accountable relationships amongst all the family members.

However, this vision soon clashed with John's personal preferences. Friday-night family takeaway and movie night coincided with John's Friday-night feature-sports game, midweek afternoon activities with the kids after school clashed with his desire to work extra hours to push for a promotion at work, and Sunday-afternoon coffee catchups with his wife fell right in the middle of his only available time to get on his beloved timber lathe in the workshop.

John's desire to see his vision come to pass meant that he started to align his priorities to serve this calling, and his personal preferences, while not in any way wrong, started to take a back seat: the timber lathe started to gather a little more dust, he caught the scores of the game on the internet Saturday morning rather than watching the whole game Friday night, and he checked out of the office at 5 every day so he could stay involved with his kids' after-school activities.

Reflecting on his choices, John commented that 'after a while, I really didn't miss those things I gave up anyway, even though at the time they seemed so important to me. I know I'm investing my time into something much more valuable than my own projects and goals'.

Hindrances to Developing Self-Governance

If we are not able to overcome these limiting forces listed below, they will continue to impact our ability to grow in character, maturity and self-governance.

i. **The inability to receive truth about our identity and purpose**

What we believe about our identity and purpose has a dramatic impact on our ability to move into a lifestyle of self-governance. That's because our lifestyle and behaviour is the physical manifestation of the internal, unseen beliefs we hold about ourselves.

We will always struggle to maintain a lifestyle that contradicts the view we have chosen to believe about ourself.

The identity of an individual is essentially a function of our choices, rather than the discovery of an immutable attribute.
—Amartya Sen

ii. **The lack of access to truth about our identity and purpose**

Sometimes we just have not had the people or resources to provide us positive, accurate information about who we are, our value and our potential. This can create a void inside of us, like missing pieces of a jigsaw puzzle.

We know what we are, but not what we may be.
—Shakespeare

iii. **The inability to take personal responsibility**

We can never address our thoughts or behaviours if we don't take responsibility that they are ours.

The prime minister of Australia cannot govern over a citizen of Indonesia living in Indonesia. In the same way, we cannot govern over an area of our life if we always see our habit, pain or reaction as someone else's fault or issue.

> *Nothing so conclusively proves a man's ability to lead others as what he does from day to day to lead himself.*
> —Thomas J. Watson

iv. Inaccurate interpretation of current circumstances

The only thing real to us is what we perceive is real.

If we see the issues and situations of our life as insurmountable—believing we can never rise above them—they will continue to define us and determine our future. We remain governed by them.

By accurately interpreting situations and seeing ourselves and circumstances in a different light, we can discover the ability to see with fresh eyes and define a new reality.

> *If you change the way you look at things, the things you look at change.*
> —Wayne Dyer

v. Failing to recognise the power of choice

The most significant power in history any individual has ever been given is the power of choice. If we do not recognise that we always have a choice, we live as slaves, as people who are powerless to see or take alternatives.

The greatest lie selfishness tells us is that we cannot choose and we, therefore, cannot rise above its control. Once we begin to exercise our right to choose, we gather a momentum and energy in our lives that move us from a place of bondage to a place of victory.

vi. Embedded habits and patterns

Sometimes patterns and habits become so ingrained in us that they prevent us from adopting upgraded, self-governing behaviours. We can mistakenly believe they are part of our character, our personality, as it becomes indistinguishable where 'we' start and the habits stop.

First, we form habits, then they form us.
Conquer your bad habits or they will conquer you.
—Rob Gilbert

We cannot imagine or fathom an existence without them, which prevents anything new and potentially more beneficial being developed in our life.

We are all inherently creatures of habit. Our life can become so strongly shaped by routines that the ability to break out of them progressively diminishes.

Instead of governing over our habits, they can govern over us.

vii. The inability to leave personal and group cultures

Everyone is connected to a range of cultures. These cultures set boundaries, limitations and expectations on our behaviour, lifestyle and standards. The degree to which we are attached to these cultures—family, community, organisation, society and even personal—determines the level of influence they have on our lifestyle and decision-making.

If we want to be self-governing, we need to be willing to move away from all competing cultures and agendas that want to govern our lives. That way, we are free to embody the values we have chosen, run toward our goal and fulfil our mission.

viii. Past wounds and hurts

When others hurt us, our heart can become damaged and we can carry a soul wound, which can determine what we fear, where our boundaries in relationships are and how we see others and ourselves.

To become a self-governing person, though, means that we ultimately have to find a way to rise above that pain, despite the reality of it, and move forward. Otherwise, it rules over us, and we are not free to pursue others-focused activities, as we are still protecting or nurturing our pain.

The Freedom In Self-Governance

Many people have a preconceived idea that a life of self-discipline and self-governance is one full of arduous rules, painfully denying our natural human expression in isolation and loneliness, but the truth is quite the opposite.

When we are self-governing, we are not obliged to pander to the extreme or harmful demands of our selfishness.

No man is free who is not master of himself
—Epictetus

When we have chosen to be governed by a set of values or principles that supersedes selfishness, we are free to respond to events, circumstances and people unencumbered by the negative, damaging motives a self-focused nature may wish us to pursue.

Joanne refuses to be offended by others, so she lives free from the poison of offence operating in our life. Simon ignores the temptation his job offers of making money illegally, so he is free from the power of corruption. Georgia is able to let go of the burning agenda of competition that used to drive her to be 'number one', so is free to delegate to others, generously serving people around her and celebrating their success.

Developing the ability to walk in the dimension of self-governance is crucial for us as leaders. When we do, our life becomes immune to the snare of internal selfish ambition and protected from the lure of external offers and opportunities.

The Progressive Impact of Self-Governance

The further we advance toward a lifestyle of self-governance, the more this governing spirit that has been fostered inside us progressively affects the environment around us, as described below.

i. Self-governance affects us as an individual

Self-governance begins on the inside of us and grows as we develop the capacity to rule over our emotions, thoughts, desires, habits, behaviours and circumstances.

ii. Self-governance affects our presentation and personal environment

Areas of our life—such as our personal grooming, and the tidiness in our home—start to be affected by growth in self-governance.

> *As we develop new beliefs about who we are,
> our behaviour will change to support
> the new identity.*
> —Anthony Robbins

Leaving the dirty dishes in the sink or spending a whole day watching TV, which were once completely normal behaviours to us, may now seem out of place, inconsistent with our revised values, identity and sense of purpose.

iii. **Self-governance affects those connected to us**

As we demonstrate a heightened value and sensitivity for others that supersedes our former self-focused approach to people, our relationships are all positively affected.

We may commit to higher levels of accountability and be open to mentoring and input from those we trust.

We are also able to assist and empower others on their own journey of self-governance.

iv. **Self-governance affects the structures we are in**

Previously, we were willingly compliant in submitting to the status quo, but now are resistant to flowing with accepted norms, even if the majority endorses them.

> *Tolerance is the virtue of the man without convictions.*
> —G. K Chesterton

To relieve the tension of this clash of cultures, we are likely to try to change it from within, or leave and pioneer a work of our own, aligned with our values.

v. **Self-governance affects our community**

The self-governance established and still growing inside us impacts across business, family, politics, media, education and community domains.

Where we see the community being influenced in a way contrary to our vision, values and culture, our inner conviction is so strong that we are likely to start to speak out publicly to share our view, engage with the ruling bodies directly, lobby for change or present the community with alternative choices.

We are so connected to the goals of our vision, and our identity is shaped so strongly by the values we have submitted to, that we are not prepared to be governed by any other philosophy, structure or culture.

CHAPTER ELEVEN

The Journey Ahead

Leadership is a journey and a process. Leaders are made, not born. Wherever you are in your leadership journey or whatever your primary vocation is—whether you're a parent, a staff member in an organisation, a CEO or an elected politician—that's the environment you are currently called to influence through your leadership.

You can experience your leadership upgrade and bring positive transformation to your environment!

This offer is conditional, however, on us embarking on the process of character development, being open to receiving input, and assessing our motivations as we pursue the leadership mandate.

Leadership Upgrade Declarations

When we begin the journey of adopting the characteristics and values detailed in the preceding chapters, we will begin to experience our *leadership upgrade.*

You can use these statements below as declarations about the type of person and leader you are becoming as you adopt and apply the contents of each chapter. Say these daily, or as often as you feel the need, to help align your thinking and beliefs to move forward.

1. I carry a high level of integrity in all my dealings. I'm accountable to others, particularly in relationships and finances. I proactively address issues that can undermine the values and standards I have set within my sphere of influence.
2. I carry a strong belief about who I am and what my purpose is. I am not a leader of convenience; I am a leader of conviction—led by my internal sense of assignment, not external rewards.
3. I'm not confined to the current situation but can see the potential and possibilities of a preferred future. I'm anchored to a vision of a preferred reality, which energises me to move beyond limitations, communicating what I see to others and connecting them to the process of bringing it to reality.
4. I prioritise relationships above success, always prepared to say sorry to restore relationships, and my leadership is people focused. I'm honourable to mentors, transparent with my peers and invested in my protégés.
5. I've got a toughness to continue, even when things become difficult. My persistence is a foundation for others to stand on. I keep going until something in me or around me gives way to enable me to proceed forward.
6. I recognise that time is short, so I'm building for tomorrow today. I look to connect with and shape recipients of the legacy I carry, providing them the input and insight to run their leg of the relay race.

7. I serve those connected to me through an attitude of love and care, and the tangible act of giving my time, resources and energy. I've made my own immediate needs of lower priority than contributing to the vision I am pursuing and people I am serving.
8. I'm willing to pioneer, by breaking through conformity and facing conflict to continue a lifestyle of growth. I continually expand my internal capacity while influencing the status quo in the environment.
9. I have trained my mind to support my dreams, receive truth and reject negativity, knowing that *if I change my thoughts, I change my life*. I have built a mental strength that allows me to interpret circumstances accurately and face setbacks constructively. My thoughts are my ally, not my enemy.
10. I am leading myself before I look to lead anyone else. I have identified and begun a journey of rising above selfishness, ambition and the potential negative effects of power on my life. I am developing this in my personal life so that it manifests in my public leadership. I am moving to a place where I am governed by the values and principles associated with my vision.

The Journey Begins!

When we compare ourselves against these statements of the ideal version of ourselves, we may fall short. Of course, we all will.

But for the sake of our families, workplaces and communities, we must pursue them if we are to answer the call to become more accurate leaders, more capable of carrying the leadership mandate and better equipped to bring positive transformation to our environment.

There is both a need and a call for a new generation of leaders to capture these characteristics, develop them in the privacy of their personal lives and demonstrate them in the public arena.

This call extends to people just like you, whether it's in the home, the workplace or the community domain. It's most likely all three.

A new breed of leaders will arise in the season ahead, who model a counterculture to the typical leaders we have observed in recent times. They will be easily identified, will reset the public expectation of the quality of leaders sought in the future, and will reshape their environment.

I hope to see you among them.

Keep growing, and keep leading!

Michael Rowell

Acknowledgements

Thank you to Helen and Grace for allowing me the time to invest in completing this book. I could not have done it without you!

About the Author

Michael has been leading individuals, groups and organisations in a range of industries and environments for over 25 years. He holds a Master of Leadership degree from the University of New England and is passionate about seeing people's leadership capacity grow and their level of influence develop.

A strong believer in the power of leadership to positively impact individuals, families, organisations and community, he is highly effective at communicating proven, practical leadership concepts that can be applied immediately to bring positive change. You will find him a supportive, insightful and effective facilitator committed to seeing you succeed (and enjoying a laugh along the way!).

When he's not getting schooled at Connect 4 by his eleven-year-old daughter or spending much more time on his DIY projects than the instructional videos suggest, he is working on his leadership and followership, and helpings others do the same.

Next Steps

If you've enjoyed the content in this book, you can stay connected with me to

- learn more about my training programs
- receive leadership content
- stay up to date about future publications
- discuss personal coaching
- or just to chat about your current leadership situations ... I'd love to hear what's happening with you in your world!

Simply email me at michael@empowerednation.com.au and we'll be able to stay in touch.

Can You Help?
Thank You for Reading My Book!

I really appreciate all your feedback, and I love hearing what you have to say.

I need your input to make the next version of this book and my future books better.

Please leave me an honest review online where you purchased your copy and let me know what you thought of the book.

Thanks so much!

Michael Rowell

Endnotes

[1] Robert Lussier and Christopher Achua, Leadership Theory, Application & Skill Development, Mason, Ohio: South-Western Cengage Learning, 2013, 374–75.

[2] Ronald Burke, 'Why Leaders Fail: Exploring the Darkside', https://doi.org/10.1108/01437720610652862.

[3] Lussier and Achua, Leadership: Theory, Application, & Skill, 326–27.

[4] Troy Segal, 'Enron Scandal: The Fall of a Wall Street Darling', https://www.investopedia.com/updates/enron-scandal-summary/; Permanent Subcommittee on Investigations of the Committee on Governmental Affairs United States Senate, 'The Role of The Board of Directors in Enron's Collapse', https://www.govinfo.gov/content/pkg/CPRT-107SPRT80393/pdf/CPRT-107SPRT80393.pdf.

[5] Unbelievable Facts, '10 Outrageous Cases of Leaders Abusing Their Power', https://unbelievable-facts.com/2018/01/leaders-abusing-their-power.html.

[6] Jefferson Tang, 'Bronwyn King: From Disappointments to Melbournian of the Year', https://www.eternalpossibilities.com.au/posts/bronwyn-king; Gideon Haigh, 'The Doctor Who Beat Big Tobacco', https://www.theguardian.com/news/2016/aug/01/the-doctor-who-beat-big-tobacco.

https://www.theguardian.com/news/2016/aug/01/the-doctor-who-beat-big-tobacco.

[7] Jenny, 'Successful Women: Australia's First Commercial Pilot Was a Teenage girl!' https://www.goagainsttheflow.org.au/successful-women-australias-first-commercial-pilot-teenage-girl/; Wikipedia, 'Nancy Bird Walton', https://en.wikipedia.org/wiki/Nancy_Bird_Walton.

[8] Malala Fund, https://www.malala.org/malalas-story; Caitlin O'Connell, '15 Ordinary People Who Changed History', Reader's Digest, https://www.rd.com/list/inspiring-stories-9-ordinary-people-who-changed-history/; 'The Nobel Peace Prize for 2014, https://www.nobelprize.org/prizes/peace/2014/press-release/.

[9] History, 'MADD founder's daughter killed by drunk driver', https://www.history.com/this-day-in-history/madd-founders-daughter-killed-by-drunk-driver; Biography, 'Candy Lightner', https://www.biography.com/activist/candy-lightner.

[10] Alison Coleman, 'Why Mentors Can be the Making of Entrepreneurs like Branson', https://www.forbes.com/sites/alisoncoleman/2016/04/10/why-mentors-can-be-the-making-of-entrepreneurs-like-branson/?sh=548d9b541778.

[11] Burt Nanus, Visionary Leadership: Creating a Compelling Sense of Direction for Your Organization, San Francisco: Jossey-Bass, 1992. The last paragraph is taken from Jacqueline Martin, Brendan McCormack, Donna Fitzsimons and Rebecca Spirig, 'The Importance of Inspiring a Shared Vision', International Practice Development Journal, 4:2 (2014), 11, who are summarizing the book.

[12] Brian O'Reilly, 'The Mechanic Who Fixed Continental', https://archive.fortune.com/magazines/fortune/fortune_archive/1999/12/20/270531/index.htm; Wendy Zellner, 'Lucky or Smart, Gordon Bethune Has Continental Climbing', https://www.bloomberg.com/news/articles/1996-05-26/lucky-or-smart-gordon-bethune-has-continental-climbing.

[13] Kim Clark, 'Gordon Bethune: The Man Who Turned Continental Airlines Around', https://www.avgeekery.com/avgeek-spotlight-gordon-bethune-former-ceo-continental-airlines/#:~:text=Prior%20to%20Bethune%20coming%20on,bankruptcy%20not%20once%2C%20but%20twice.

[14] Jessica Naziri, 'Turnaround CEOs', https://www.cnbc.com/2011/11/30/Turnaround-CEOs.html.

[15] SoftSchools.com, 'I Have A Dream Speech', https://www.softschools.com/facts/us_history/i_have_a_dream_speech_facts/1341/; Wikipedia, 'I Have A Dream', https://en.wikipedia.org/wiki/I_Have_a_Dream.

[16] Mary Bagley, 'George Washington Carver: Biography, Inventions & Quotes'.

[17] Anthony Botibol, '4 examples of customer insight improving sales and marketing performance', https://www.bluevenn.com/blog/why-customer-insight-marketing-can-be-a-powerful-sales-tool.

[18] Ben Hardy, 'Destroy Negativity from Your Mind with This Simple Exercise', https://medium.com/the-mission/a-practical-hack-to-combat-negative-thoughts-in-2-minutes-or-less-cc3d1bddb3af#:~:text=According%20to%20the%20National%20Science,than%20we%20think%20positive%20thoughts.

[19] Ready, 'Why Great Leaders Focus on Mastering Relationships', https://sloanreview.mit.edu/article/why-great-leaders-focus-on-mastering-relationships/.

[20] Unified Lawyers, 'Divorce Rate by Country: The World's 10 Most and Least Divorced Nations, https://www.unifiedlawyers.com.au/blog/global-divorce-rates-statistics/.

[21] Hara Estroff Marano, 'The Dangers of Loneliness', Psychology Today, July 1, 2003. https://www.psychologytoday.com/au/articles/200307/the-dangers-loneliness.

[22] Richard Martin, 'Relationship as a Core of Effective Leadership', Low Intensity Conflict & Law Enforcement, 13: 3 (2013), 76-85, https://www.researchgate.net/publication/273769080_Relationship_as_a_Core_of_Effective_Leadership.

[23] Relationships Foundation, 'Cost of Family Failure: £47 bn and still rising', Feb. 14, 2015, https://relationshipsfoundation.org/news/cost-of-family-failure-47-bn-and-still-rising/.

[24] Dr. Lester Coleman, 'Understanding couple relationship breakdown: impacts, protective factors, relationship difficulties and interventions designed to support parents during the transition to first-time parenting', https://pdfs.semanticscholar.org/0ea5/a54ce2e7ced67de2589fe3fea85c104389ac.pdf.

[25] Harvey Dubin, 'Speaking and Listening Are Action', https://www.jmw.com/blog/productivity-making-results-happen-part-2/.

[26] Travis Bradberry, '8 Secrets of Great Communicators', https://www.forbes.com/sites/travisbradberry/2016/07/19/8-secrets-of-great-communicators/?sh=7b3bdb383029.

[27] Dustin Smith, 'Nonverbal Communication: How Body Language & Nonverbal Cues Are Key', https://www.lifesize.com/en/video-conferencing-blog/speaking-without-words#:~:text=There%20have%20been%20a%20number,Mehrabian%20in%20the%201960s.

[28] Dr. Jonathon David, Global Leadership Summit 2015 Lecture.

[29] Book Authority, '83 Best Persistence Books of All Time', https://bookauthority.org/books/best-persistence-books.

[30] Leah Fessler, ' "You're No Genius": Her father's shutdowns made Angela Duckworth a world expert on grit', https://qz.com/work/1233940/angela-duckworth-explains-grit-is-the-key-to-success-and-self-confidence/.

[31] Amazon.com.au, 'Grit: The Power of Passion and Perseverance', New York: Scribner Book Company; Illustrated edition, 2016.

[32] Your Dictionary, https://quotes.yourdictionary.com/author/quotes/611132.

[33] Bethany Lape, 'Henry Ford's Bankruptcies Offer Lessons in Persistence', https://www.myhorizontoday.com/bankruptcy101/henry-fords-bankruptcies-offer-lessons-in-persistence/; Wikipedia, 'Ford Model T', https://en.wikipedia.org/wiki/Ford_Model_T.

[34] Biography, Walt Disney's Rocky Road to Success, https://www.biography.com/news/walt-disney-failures; Wikipedia, 'Walt Disney', https://en.wikipedia.org/wiki/Walt_Disney.

[35] Stephan Evans, 'Sewol ferry: S Korea Court Gives Captain Life Sentence for Murder', https://www.bbc.com/news/world-asia-32492263; Jethro Mullen, 'Abandon Ship? In recent maritime disasters, captains don't hang around', https://edition.cnn.com/2014/04/21/world/asia/ship-captain-role/index.html.

[36] Christina Desmarais, 'Science Says the Most Successful Kids Have Parents Who Do These 5 Things', https://www.inc.com/christina-desmarais/science-says-most-successful-kids-have-parents-who-do-these-5-things_2.html.

[37] History, 'U.S. Hockey Team Beats the Soviets in the "Miracle on Ice"', https://www.history.com/this-day-in-history/u-s-hockey-team-makes-miracle-on-ice; Movie Quotes, ' "Miracle" Quotes (2004)', https://www.moviequotes.com/s-movie/miracle/.

[38] Stuart James, 'Leicester City's Title Triumph: The Inside Story of an Extraordinary Season', https://www.theguardian.com/football/2016/may/03/leicester-city-title-inside-story-premier-league-champions-claudio-ranieri.

[39] Wikipedia, 'The Rumble in the Jungle', https://en.wikipedia.org/wiki/The_Rumble_in_the_Jungle; 'CoolBet, Sports Underdogs: 10 Greatest Stories of All Time', https://coolbet.co/sports-underdogs-10-greatest-stories-of-all-time/.

[40] Wikipedia, 'Persistence (psychology)', https://en.wikipedia.org/wiki/Persistence_(psychology)'.

[41] N. T. Feather, 'The Study of Persistence', https://doi.org/10.1037/h0042645.

[42] Vanessa Bennett, 'Some People Persist and Others Don't ... Here's Why', https://nextevolutionperformance.com/2018/07/some-people-persist-and-others-dont-heres-why/.

43 Dick Kazan, 'Abraham Lincoln: A remarkable story of perseverance', http://www.kazantoday.com/WeeklyArticles/abraham-lincoln.html; Inspiration Boost, 'Lincoln's Famous. Failures', https://i.pinimg.com/originals/32/ea/13/32ea13e779837576085eac75029313f9.jpg.

44 Nathan Furr, 'How Failure Taught Edison to Repeatedly Innovate', https://www.forbes.com/sites/nathanfurr/2011/06/09/how-failure-taught-edison-to-repeatedly-innovate/?sh=3f1d160065e9.

45 The Franklin Institute, 'Edisons Lightbulb', https://www.fi.edu/history-resources/edisons-lightbulb.

46 Rats of Tobruk Association, 'Why the Name 'Rats of Tobruk?' http://www.ratsoftobrukassociation.org.au/index_htm_files/Why%20the%20Name.jpg; Australian War Memorial, 'Rats of Tobruk 1941', https://www.awm.gov.au/visit/exhibitions/tobruk.

47 Convict Creations, 'Rats of Tobruk', http://www.convictcreations.com/history/tobruk.htm.

48 AZ Quotes, https://www.azquotes.com/author/12582-Erwin_Rommel.

49 Dr. Diane Hamilton, 'The Rare Values for Leadership with Hellicy Ng'ambi', https://drdianehamilton.com/the-rare-values-for-leadership-with-hellicy-ngambi/; Bank of Zambia 'Prof. Hellicy C. Ng'ambi', https://www.boz.zm/about/prof-hellicy-c-ng-ambi-bio.htm; Linked In, 'Overcoming Obstacles: 12 Inspiring Stories of Success', https://www.linkedin.com/pulse/overcoming-obstacles-12-inspiring-stories-success-dr-diane-hamilton.

50 Australian HR Institute, 'Succession Planning', https://www.ahri.com.au/resources/ahriassist/hr-strategies-and-planning/workforce-planning/succession-planning/.

51 McKinsey Quarterly, 'Staying One Step Ahead at Pixar: An Interview with Ed Catmull', https://www.mckinsey.com/business-functions/organization/our-insights/staying-one-step-ahead-at-pixar-an-interview-with-ed-catmull#.

52 Collins Dictionary, 'Honour', https://www.collinsdictionary.com/dictionary/english/honour.

53 'Slaves and Slavery', Jewish Encyclopedia, http://www.jewishencyclopedia.com/articles/13799-slaves-and-slavery.

54 Rakesh Krishnan Simha, 'The Men Who Starved to Death to Save the World's Seeds', https://www.rbth.com/blogs/2014/05/12/the_men_who_

Leadership Upgrade

starved_to_death_to_save_the_worlds_seeds_35135#:~:text=During%20the%20siege%20of%20Leningrad,for%20a%20post%2Dapocalyptic%20world.

55 Australian War Memorial, 'History of Anzac Day', https://www.awm.gov.au/commemoration/anzac-day/traditions; https://en.wikipedia.org/wiki/Anzac_Day#Commemoration_in_other_countries.

56 Kim Renfro, 'Watch Oscar Winner Regina King Thank Her Mother', https://www.insider.com/regina-king-oscar-speech-video-2019-2.

57 Wikipedia, 'Wilma Rudolph', https://en.wikipedia.org/wiki/Wilma_Rudolph;

Biography, 'Wilma Rudolph', https://www.biography.com/athlete/wilma-rudolph;

She Made History, 'Her Story: Wilma Rudolph', http://shemadehistory.com/her-story-wilma-rudolph/;

Encycopedia.com, 'Wilma Rudolph 1940—', https://www.encyclopedia.com/people/sports-and-games/sports-biographies/wilma-rudolph.

58 Wikipedia, 'James Gobbo', https://en.wikipedia.org/wiki/James_Gobbo#:~:text=Gobbo%20served%20as%20Lieutenant%2DGovernor,state%20governor%20of%20Italian%20descent.

59 Robert K Greenleaf, 'Center for Servant Leadership', https://www.greenleaf.org/what-is-servant-leadership/.

60 Greenleaf Centre (Asia) for Servant Leadership, 'Scientific Research on Servant Leadership', http://www.greenleafasia.org/scientific-research-on-servant-leadership.html.

61 Sidney Myer Fund, 'About Us', https://www.myerfoundation.org.au/about-us; Wikipedia, 'Sidney Myer' https://en.wikipedia.org/wiki/Sidney_Myer; Australian Dictionary of Biography, 'Myer, Simcha (Sidney) (1878–1934).

62 Wikipedia, 'Mother Teresa', https://en.wikipedia.org/wiki/Mother_Teresa#cite_note-71;

Leona Salazar, 'Lights Out for Mother Teresa', https://bernardgoldberg.com/lights-out-for-mother-teresa/; Biography, 'Mother Teresa', https://www.biography.com/religious-figure/mother-teresa.

63 Wikipedia, 'Socrates', https://en.wikipedia.org/wiki/Socrates#Beliefs.

[64] Wikipedia, 'International Cultic Studies Association', https://en.wikipedia.org/wiki/International_Cultic_Studies_Association.

[65] Steve Eichel, 'The Mind of the Fanatic', http://www.dreichel.com/Articles/fanaticism.htm.

[66] HRD Memorial, 'Celebrating Those Who Were Killed Defending Human Rights', https://hrdmemorial.org/hrdrecord/galina-starovoytova/.

[67] John Rice, Graham Hubbard, Peter Galvin, Strategic Management: Thinking, Analysis, Action, Pearson, Australia: Frenchs Forest, 389–90, 2015.

[68] Biography, 'Martin Luther', https://www.biography.com/religious-figure/martin-luther; BBC, 'History: Martin Luther (1483–1546)', BBC – History – Historic Figures: Martin Luther (1483-1546); Britannica, 'Martin Luther Later Years', https://www.britannica.com/biography/Martin-Luther/Later-years.

[69] Strategy + Business, 'Transforming a Traditional Bank into an Agile Market Leader', https://www.Strategy-Business.Com/Article/Transforming-A-Traditional-Bank-Into-An-Agile-Market-Leader?Gko=036bf.

[70] 'Love a Quote', https://loveaquote.com/leaders-are-fascinated-by-future.-you-are-a-leader-if-marcus-buckingham/.

[71] ManUp, 'Real Stories Grant Douglas', https://www.manup.org.nz/realstories.

[72] Sean Meehan, 'How Breakthrough Leadership Can Defy Company Death', https://www.imd.org/contentassets/0cfe9dd762c8474fa92bc171a615a022/tc065-16---breakthrough-leadership-pdf.pdf.

[73] Arati Carroll, 'Why Peter Drucker Hailed Francis Hesselbein as the World's Best Leader?' https://economictimes.indiatimes.com/why-peter-drucker-hailed-francis-hesselbein-as-the-worlds-best-leader/articleshow/5446959.cms; Strategy + Business, 'Frances Hesselbein's Merit Badge in Leadership', https://www.strategy-business.com/article/00332?gko=0957c.

[74] BBC Sport, 'Formula 1's Greatest Drivers. Number 2: Juan Manuel Fangio', https://www.bbc.com/sport/formula1/20258984.

[75] Joost, 'How Real Leaders Melt the Iceberg of Ignorance with Humility', https://corporate-rebels.com/iceberg-of-ignorance/.

[76] 'Capacity', online dictionary, https://www.google.com/search?q=capacity+define&rlz=1C1GCEA_enAU781AU781&oq=capacity+define&aqs=chrome..69i57j69i59l2j69i60l5.2334j0j9&sourceid=chrome&ie=UTF-8.What.

[77] Roger Trapp, 'Why Leaders Need to Be Positive Thinkers', https://www.forbes.com/sites/rogertrapp/2014/01/31/leaders-need-to-be-positive-thinkers/?sh=62c35e2d4e01.

[78] Daily Good, 'Overcoming the Brain's Negativity Bias', https://www.dailygood.org/story/2453/overcoming-the-brain-s-negativity-bias-jill-suttie/.

[79] Be Brain Fit, 'Automatic Negative Thoughts (ANTS): How To Break The Habit', https://bebrainfit.com/automatic-negative-thoughts/; The Miracle Zone, '80% of Thoughts Are Negative…95% Are Repetitive', https://faithhopeandpsychology.wordpress.com/2012/03/02/80-of-thoughts-are-negative-95-are-repetitive/; Prakhar Verma, 'Destroy Negativity From Your Mind With This Simple Exercise', https://medium.com/the-mission/a-practical-hack-to-combat-negative-thoughts-in-2-minutes-or-less-cc3d1bddb3af; Cognitive Health Group, 'Obsessive Thinking, Worry, Rumination – Cognitive Behavior Therapy (CBT)', https://cognitive-behavior-therapy.com/cognitive-behavior-therapy-for-obsessivethinking-worry-rumination; Dr. Raj Raghunathan, 'How Negative Is Your 'Mental Chatter?', How Negative is Your "Mental Chatter"? | Psychology Today.

[80] HealthLine, 'Negative Thinking Can Harm Your Brain and Increase Your Dementia Risk', https://www.healthline.com/health-news/negative-thinking-can-harm-brain-increase-dementia-risk#:~:text=In%20a%20new%20study%2C%20researchers,a%20greater%20risk%20of%20dementia.

[81] The Arsenio Buck Show, 'Seven Ways to Cultivate a Mental Attitude That Will Bring You Peace & Happiness', https://thearseniobuckshow.com/2017/09/06/seven-ways-to-cultivate-a-mental-attitude-that-will-bring-you-peace-happiness/.

[82] Steve McVey, 'Critical Thinking Skills for Leadership Development' 2:4 (1995), 86–97, https://journals.sagepub.com/doi/pdf/10.1177/107179199500200407, The Journal of Leadership Studies.

[83] 99 Hills, 'How to Train An Elephant', How to Train an Elephant—99 Hills; Ryan Holmes, 'The Elephant and the Rope: One Mental Trick to Unlock Your Growth', https://www.inc.com/ryan-holmes/the-elephant-and-the-rope-one-mental-trick-to-unlock-your-growth.html; Brandon Telg, 'Dr. Jaron Jones, & Carly Barnes, 'Break Your Invisible Chains: Own the Power of Your Story', http://frank.jou.ufl.edu/wp-content/uploads/2016/09/booksample.pdf.

[84] Jill Suttie, 'Overcoming the Brain's Negativity Bias', https://www.dailygood.org/story/2453/overcoming-the-brain-s-negativity-bias/.

85 Roy Baumeister, Ellen Bratslavsky, Catrin Finkenauer and Kathleen Vohs, 'Bad is Stronger Than Good', https://doi.org/10.1037/1089-2680.5.4.323.

86 Amrisha Vaish, Tobias Grossmann, Amanda Woodward, 'Not All Emotions Are Created Equal: The negativity bias in social-emotional development', doi: 10.1037/0033-2909.134.3.383.

87 T. Ito, J. Larsen, N. Smith and J. Cacioppo, 'Negative Information Weighs More Heavily on the Brain: The negativity bias in evaluative categorizations', doi: 10.1037//0022-3514.75.4.887.

88 Chris Kresser, 'How to Hardwire Happiness', with Dr. Rick Hanson, https://chriskresser.com/how-to-hardwire-happiness-with-dr-rick-hanson/; Blake Thorne, 'Why Your Brain Has a Negativity Bias and How to Fix It', http://blog.idonethis.com/negativity-bias/.

89 John Brandon, 'Science says There's a Simply Reason You Keep Thinking Negative Thoughts All Day', https://www.inc.com/john-brandon/science-says-theres-a-simple-reason-you-keep-thinking-negative-thoughts-all-day.html.

90 Blake Thorne, 'Why Your Brain Has a Negativity Bias and How to Fix It', http://blog.idonethis.com/negativity-bias/.

91 Candice Georgiadas, '10 Successful Leaders Share Their Struggles with Imposter Syndrome and How to Overcome It', https://www.entrepreneur.com/slideshow/345415; Wikipedia, 'Kim Perrell', https://en.wikipedia.org/wiki/Kim_Perell.

92 Candice Georgiadas, '10 Successful Leaders Share Their Struggles with Imposter Syndrome and How to Overcome It', https://www.entrepreneur.com/slideshow/345415.

93 History.com, Florence Nightingale' 'https://www.history.com/topics/womens-history/florence-nightingale-1; Nicole Garner, '15 Famous People Who Picked Careers Their Parents Disapproved Of',

https://www.mentalfloss.com/article/72361/15-famous-people-who-picked-careers-their-parents-disapproved.

94 Arash Asli, '6 Tips for Growing with an Entrepreneurial Mindset', https://www.forbes.com/sites/theyec/2018/05/25/6-tips-for-growing-with-an-entrepreneurial-mindset/?sh=4a9bf4831343.

95 Roger Trapp, 'Why Leaders Need to Be Positive Thinkers', https://www.forbes.com/sites/rogertrapp/2014/01/31/leaders-need-to-be-positive-thinkers/?sh=62c35e2d4e01.

⁹⁶ Courtney Ackerman, 'What is Neuroplasticity? A Psychologist Explains', https://positivepsychology.com/neuroplasticity/.

⁹⁷ Dr, Caroline Leaf, 'You Are Not a Victim of Your Biology', https://drleaf.com/blogs/news/you-are-not-a-victim-of-your-biology.

⁹⁸ Duquesne University, 'The Pygmalion Effect', https://www.duq.edu/about/centers-and-institutes/center-for-teaching-excellence/teaching-and-learning-at-duquesne/pygmalion.

⁹⁹ Positive Psychology.com, '40+ Benefits of Self-Control and Self-Discipline', https://positivepsychology.com/benefits-self-control-discipline/.

¹⁰⁰ Dave Ferguson: The Leader's Coach, 'Leadership: Should You Be Selfish or Selfless?' https://livingtolead.com/tag/selfless-leader/.

¹⁰¹ Journey to Leadership blog.com 'The Importance of Becoming a Self-Disciplined Leader', https://journeytoleadershipblog.com/2019/11/11/importance-becoming-self-disciplined-leader/#:~:text=Leaders%20use%20self%2Ddiscipline%20to,themselves%20and%20place%20boundaries%2C%20to.

¹⁰² Carey Nieuwhof, '10 Signs Your Leadership Is Driven by Selfish Ambition', https://careynieuwhof.com/10-signs-your-leadership-is-driven-by-selfish-ambition/.

¹⁰³ Marcel Schwantes. 'If You're Too Busy for These 3 Things, Your Leadership Skills May Need a Tune-Up: This Will Reveal the Leader's True Intent', https://www.inc.com/marcel-schwantes/if-youre-too-busy-for-these-3-things-your-leadership-skills-may-need-a-tune-up.html.

¹⁰⁴ Janelle Spence, 'Servant Leader vs. Selfish Leader—and Why It Matters: How Motives Affect Your Business', https://centennialinc.com/centennial-blog/servant-leader-vs-selfish-leader-and-why-it-matters/.

¹⁰⁵ Prudy Gourguechon, 'A Neglected But Essential Leadership Trait—Why Self-Control Really Matters', https://www.forbes.com/sites/prudygourguechon/2018/04/03/a-neglected-but-essential-leadership-trait-why-self-control-really-matters/?sh=569153d3787a.

¹⁰⁶ Exploring Your Mind, '5 Traits of Emotionally Immature People', 5 Traits of Emotionally Immature People – Exploring your mind.

¹⁰⁷ Victor Lipman, 'If Your Boss Shows These 4 Signs, Head For The Hills', https://www.forbes.com/sites/victorlipman/2017/06/07/if-your-boss-shows-these-4-signs-head-for-the-hills/?sh=8af45633699e; Carey Nieu-

whof, '10 Signs Your Leadership Is Driven By Selfish Ambition', https://careynieuwhof.com/10-signs-your-leadership-is-driven-by-selfish-ambition/.

[108] Jennifer Crocker, Amy Canavella and Ashley Brown, 'Social Motivation: Costs and Benefits of Selfishness and Otherishness', https://doi.org/10.1146/annurev-psych-010416-044145.

[109] James Sonne and Don Gash, 'Psychopathy to Altruism: Neurobiology of the Selfish–Selfless Spectrum', doi: 10.3389/fpsyg.2018.00575.

[110] Henri Santos, Michael Varnum, Igor Grossmann, 'Global Increases in Individualism', https://doi.org/10.1177/0956797617700622.

[111] Sarah Green Carmichael, 'The Perils of Self-Promotion', https://hbr.org/2014/01/the-perils-of-self-promotion.

[112] EurekAlert, 'UMass Researcher Finds Most People Lie in Everyday Conversation', https://www.eurekalert.org/pub_releases/2002-06/uoma-urf061002.php.

[113] EuroStat Statistics Explained, 'Marriage and Divorce Statistics', https://ec.europa.eu/eurostat/statistics-explained/index.php?title=Marriage_and_divorce_statistics#Further_Eurostat_information.

[114] Scott Shelby, Galena Rhoades, Scott Stanley, Elizabeth Allen and Howard Markman, 'Reasons for Divorce and Recollections of Premarital Intervention: Implications for Improving Relationship Education' doi: 10.1037/a0032025.

[115] S. Ali, E. Onaivi, P. Dodd, J. Cadet, S. Schenk, M. Kuhar and G. Koob, 'Understanding the Global Problem of Drug Addiction Is a Challenge for IDARS Scientists', doi: 10.2174/157015911795017245.

[116] MentalHelp.net, 'Why Don't They Just Stop? Addiction and the Loss of Control', https://www.mentalhelp.net/addiction/why-cant-they-stop/.

[117] World Health Organisation, 'Obesity and Overweight', https://www.who.int/news-room/fact-sheets/detail/obesity-and-overweight.

[118] Karol Lewczuk, Adrian Wojcik and Mateusz Gola, 'Changes in Internet Pornography Use between 2004 and 2016 in Poland', doi: 10.31234/osf.io/tmn4r.

[119] Webroot.com, 'Internet Pornography by the Numbers; A Significant Threat to Society', https://www.webroot.com/au/en/resources/tips-articles/internet-pornography-by-the-number.

[120] Maria Cohut, 'Global Alcohol Intake Has Increased by 70%, Study

Warns', https://www.medicalnewstoday.com/articles/325135.

[121] UNODC.com, 'UNODC World Drug Report 2020: Global Drug Use Rising; While COVID-19 Has Far Reaching Impact on Global Drug Markets', https://www.unodc.org/unodc/press/releases/2020/June/media-advisory---global-launch-of-the-20207-world-drug-report.html.

[122] Dr Suzi Gage, 'Is Addiction on the Rise?' https://www.sciencefocus.com/the-human-body/is-addiction-on-the-rise/.

[123] Jennifer Crocker, Amy Canavella and Ashley Brown, 'Social Motivation: Costs and Benefits of Selfishness and Otherishness', https://doi.org/10.1146/annurev-psych-010416-044145; Goop.com, 'The Legacy of a Narcissistic Parent', https://goop.com/wellness/relationships/the-legacy-of-a-narcissistic-parent/; Preston Ni, '10 Signs of a Narcissistic Parent', https://www.psychologytoday.com/au/blog/communication-success/201602/10-signs-narcissistic-parent.

[124] Goop.com, 'The Legacy of a Narcissistic Parent', https://goop.com/wellness/relationships/the-legacy-of-a-narcissistic-parent/.

[125] Laryl McBride, 'The Real Effect of Narcissistic Parenting on Children', https://www.psychologytoday.com/us/blog/the-legacy-distorted-love/201802/the-real-effect-narcissistic-parenting-children.

[126] David Witt, 'The Negative Impact of Self-Serving, Controlling Leaders', https://resources.kenblanchard.com/blanchard-leaderchat/the-negative-impact-of-self-serving-controlling-leaders.

[127] Dan Pontefract, 'The Collateral Damage of Selfish Leadership', https://www.forbes.com/sites/danpontefract/2015/01/05/the-collateral-damage-of-selfish-leadership/?sh=32c4b9d4754d.

[128] Insight News.com.au, 'Guide Dogs Boss Who Stole $210k Faces Possible 10-Year Sentence', https://www.insightnews.com.au/guide-dogs-boss-who-stole-210k-faces-possible-10-year-sentence/'; Australian Institute of Management, 'Victorian Excellence Awards Winners Announced', https://www.aim.com.au/news/victorian-excellence-awards-winners-announced.

[129] Robert Lenzner, 'The 2008 Meltdown and Where the Blame Falls', https://www.forbes.com/sites/robertlenzner/2012/06/02/the-2008-meltdown-and-where-the-blame-falls/?sh=2f562f6ea72a.

[130] Claudia Dobre, Costin Răsăuțeanu, 'Greed and Global Financial Crisis:

Reflections on the Repeal of Glass-Steagall Act', https://www.researchgate.net/publication/317684349_Greed_and_Global_Financial_Crisis_Reflections_on_the_Repeal_of_Glass-Steagall_Act.

[131] Marcel Schwantes, '10 Compelling Reasons Servant Leadership May Be the Best, Says Science', https://www.inc.com/marcel-schwantes/10-convincing-reasons-to-consider-servant-leadership-according-to-research.html.

[132] Matt Gaw, 'I Was A Selfish Dad', https://www.theguardian.com/lifeandstyle/2011/aug/27/dad-childcare-stay-at-home.

[133] Adam Grant, 'Power Doesn't Corrupt. It Just Exposes Who Leaders Really Are', https://www.washingtonpost.com/business/economy/power-doesnt-corrupt-it-just-exposes-who-leaders-really-are/2019/02/22/f5680116-3600-11e9-854a-7a14d7fec96a_story.html.

[134] Adam Grant, 'Power Doesn't Corrupt. It Just Exposes Who Leaders Really Are', Power doesn't corrupt. It just exposes who leaders really are. – The Washington Post.

[135] David Kipnis, 'Does Power Corrupt?' Journal of Personality and Social Psychology 24:1 (1972), 33–41.

[136] Association for Psychological Science, 'Entitled at the Top: Are Leaders More Selfish Than the Rest of Us?', https://www.psychologicalscience.org/news/minds-business/entitled-at-the-top-are-leaders-more-selfish-than-the-rest-of-us.html; Annika Scholl and Daan Scheepers, 'Understanding Power in Social Context: How Power Relates to Language and Communication in Line with Responsibilities or Opportunities', https://www.researchgate.net/publication/279423259_Understanding_power_in_social_context_How_power_relates_to_language_and_communication_in_line_with_responsibilities_or_opportunities.

[137] SocialScienceSpace.com, 'Why Are Some Leaders Selfish?' https://www.socialsciencespace.com/2014/04/why-are-some-leaders-selfish/.

[138] University of California Research, 'How Power Makes People Selfish', How power makes people selfish | University of California.

[139] SocialScienceSpace.com, 'Why Are Some Leaders Selfish?' https://www.socialsciencespace.com/2014/04/why-are-some-leaders-selfish/.

[140] Jon Maner and Nicole Mead, 'The Essential Tension between Leadership and Power: When Leaders Sacrifice Group Goals for the Sake of Self-Interest', Journal of Personality and Social Psychology 99: 3 (2010), 482–97, https://doi.org/10.1037/a0018559.

141 Shu-Tsen Kuo, 'A Selfish Leader Is the Product of Traits and Situation', A Selfish Leader Is the Product of Traits and Situation | Lead Read Today (osu.edu).

142 Morela Hernandez, 'Putting an End to Leaders' Self-Serving Behavior', Putting an End to Leaders' Self-Serving Behavior (mit.edu).

143 Leon Seltzer, 'Narcissism: Why It's So Rampant in Politics: Narcissist politicians don't serve the people; they serve themselves', https://www.psychologytoday.com/us/blog/evolution-the-self/201112/narcissism-why-its-so-rampant-in-politics.

144 Wikipedia, 'Eddie Obeid', https://en.wikipedia.org/wiki/Eddie_Obeid.

145 The Yale Institute of Leadership & Management, 'What Can Leaders Learn from Yale Study of Selfish Behaviour?' https://www.institutelm.com/resourceLibrary/what-can-leaders-learn-from-yale-study-of-selfish-behaviour.html.

146 American Psychological Association, 'The Essential Tension between Leadership and Power: Why Power Corrupts—and How to Prevent It', https://www.apa.org/science/about/psa/2013/10/leadership-power.

147 Iidiko Tombor, Lion Shahab, Jamie Brown, Caitlin Notley and Robert West, 'Does Non-Smoker Identity Following Quitting Predict Long-Term Abstinence? Evidence from a Population Survey in England', doi: 10.1016/j.addbeh.2015.01.026.

148 YouTube, 'Interview with Mentorloop CEO Lucy Lloyd', https://www.youtube.com/watch?v=120Ya4B_NbQ.

149 Eric Klein and Nancy Dickenson-Hazard, 'The Spirit of Mentoring', Reflections on Nursing Leadership 26: 3 (2000), 18–22, https://sigma.nursingrepository.org/handle/10755/593106.

150 Eric Klein and Nancy Dickenson-Hazard, 'The Spirit of Mentoring'. Reflections on Nursing Leadership 26: 3 (2000), 18–22.

151 Mentorloop, 'Human Reconnection: The New HR', https://mentorloop.com/mentoring-program-benefits/.

152 Mary Abbajay, 'Mentoring Matters: Three Essential Elements of Success', https://www.forbes.com/sites/maryabbajay/2019/01/20/mentoring-matters-three-essential-element-of-success/?sh=1c704a1f45a9.

153 National Academies of Sciences, Engineering and Medicine, 'The Science of Effective Mentorship in STEMM', https://doi.org/10.17226/25568.

[154] Accountable 2 You, 'Self-Accountability: Essential But Not Enough?' https://accountable2you.com/blog/self-accountability/.

[155] Dr. Jim Taylor, 'Personal Growth: Your Values, Your Life: Are you living your life in accordance with your values?' https://www.psychologytoday.com/au/blog/the-power-prime/201205/personal-growth-your-values-your-life.

[156] Dr. Jim Taylor, 'Personal Growth: How to Align Your Values and Your Life: Are your life and your values in synch?' https://www.psychologytoday.com/au/blog/the-power-prime/201205/personal-growth-how-align-your-values-and-your-life.

[157] Shideh Sedgh Bina, Jen Zimmer, 'Cone Health's Two Part Transformation', https://quarterly.insigniam.com/transformation/cone-healths-two-part-transformation/.

www.ingramcontent.com/pod-product-compliance
Lightning Source LLC
Chambersburg PA
CBHW022036290426
44109CB00014B/873